The Fabian Society

The Fabian Society has played a central role for more
development of political ideas and public policy on t..._ ..
the key challenges facing the UK and the rest of the industrialised world in a
changing society and global economy, the Society's programme aims to
explore the political ideas and the policy reforms which will define progressive
politics in the new century.

The Society is unique among think tanks in being a democratically-constituted
membership organisation. It is affiliated to the Labour Party but is editorially
and organisationally independent. Through its publications, seminars and
conferences, the Society provides an arena for open-minded public debate.

Fabian Society
11 Dartmouth Street
London SW1H 9BN
www.fabian-society.org.uk

 Fabian ideas
Editor: Adrian Harvey
Design: Rory Fisher

First published June 2001

ISBN 0 7163 0599 2
ISSN 1469 0136

British Library Cataloguing in Publication data.
A catalogue record for this book is available from the British Library.

Printed by Bell & Bain Limited, Glasgow

Contents

About the contributors

Ian Christie is associate director of the Local Futures Group and a writer and researcher on sustainable development. His latest book, with Diane Warburton, is *From Here to Sustainability: politics in the real world*, Earthscan/Real World Coalition, 2001.

Adrian Harvey is Research Director at the Fabian Society. He has been editor of *Poverty Matters* magazine, a member of the editorial board of *Benefits Journal* and has written numerous reports and articles on poverty and social inclusion.

Michael Jacobs is General Secretary of the Fabian Society, Secretary to the Commission on Taxation and Citizenship and author of its report *Paying for Progress: A New Politics of Tax for Public Spending*.

Richard Reeves is director of Futures at The Industrial Society and author of *Happy Mondays—putting the pleasure back into work*.

Sue Richards is Professor of Public Management at the University of Birmingham. She has written on public management, including cultural change, the use of markets for public service and developing an outcomes focus. She is a member of the governing body of the Audit Commission and was a member of the Government's Modernising Government Project Board.

Meg Russell is Senior Research Fellow at the Constitution Unit, University College London. She is author of *Reforming the House of Lords: Lessons from Overseas* (Oxford University Press, 2000) and numerous papers and reports.

Ken Worpole is an associate of Comedia and Demos and a leading writer on urban policy and the public realm. His latest book is *Here Comes the Sun: architecture and public space in 20th century European culture*, Reaktion, 2000.

Introduction Adrian Harvey

Early in 2001, the Fabian Society asked a number of thinkers and writers to contribute to a collection of essays, setting out their vision for the direction of a potential second term of Labour Government. Inspired by Blair's promise of 'a second term more radical than the first' at Labour's conference in 2000, the intention was to offer some signposts for how that radicalism might be achieved.

The resulting collection is the Fabian Society's contribution to the debate about where Labour goes next. The last time that the Society published a pamphlet looking forward to a second term was in May 1949. It is a mark of the scale of Labour's achievement in 2001 that, for over half a century, the Society has not published again on this theme—until now.

There is little doubting the electoral arithmetic. Labour secured a second term with its massive majority of 1997 virtually intact. Indeed, the majority was the highest ever recorded by a second term government. Plainly, Labour is in a commanding position both in terms of seats in the Commons and its share of the popular vote.

Despite this, the result is in some senses ambiguous. Turnout was its lowest for almost a century at below 60 per cent; in some areas where Labour has traditionally been strong, it dipped below 45 per cent. During the campaign, it was clear that, whilst millions were willing to give Labour the benefit of the doubt, there were signs that a third term will be much harder to win.

Clearly, 'more of the same' will not be sufficient. Labour needs to seize the opportunity presented by its majority to craft a more confident and radical programme, one which can deliver responsive public services, a just society, an open and dynamic economy, high quality of life and a vibrant democracy. Only this will both enthuse voters and capitalise on this high watermark for the left of centre.

The task demands new thinking and this pamphlet is a modest contribution to the debate to come. It presents seven essays, each setting out strategic directions and indicative policy proposals in key areas. As with all Fabian Society publications, these are the views of the individual contributors, not of the Society as a whole. But together, they offer a vision of what a more radical second term might look like across the key policy areas.

On social justice, I argue that the progress of the first term was undermined by a failure to provide clear political leadership and by insufficient regard to inequality. Labour cannot ignore income inequality; the second term needs to see measures to address the gap between rich and poor. Social justice also needs to become integral to the mainstream business of government, moving on from the approach of the first term, which was largely based on 'special measures'.

Public services were the key election issue and Labour's mandate rests on their improvement. With the planned investment scheduled, the question is one of how to deliver. Sue Richards argues that whilst many important advances have been made towards 'joining up' services and focusing on outcomes, there is much more to do. In particular, the centre must learn to 'let go' and allow front line services to use their local knowledge to deliver. And the involvement of the private sector in service delivery has to be justified by hard facts and tough analysis.

Constitutional reform was one of the quiet triumphs of the first term. But as Meg Russell argues, the programme was piecemeal and much was left undone. However, it is not simply a case of unfinished business: Labour needs to go back to the fundamentals and deliver a coherence to its democratic agenda. Electoral reform, devolution to the English regions and completing reform of the House of Lords cannot be treated in isolation, and should be the subject of a full constitutional convention.

Crucial to Labour's success in June 2001 was the stability of the economy. Now that has been achieved, argues Jonathan Michie, Government must deliver real investment in productivity and innovation to realise the goal of a modern economy, based on skills and quality, rather than low wages. Coupled with this, there is a need for corporate governance of UK firms to be improved, making stakeholding a reality.

On work, the challenge for the first term was to tackle unemployment. The task now, Richard Reeves argues, is to wage war on bad employment. Labour should encourage greater autonomy to all workers and ensure employee consultation. Government also needs to support progression within employment, so that workers do not get stuck in a cycle of low skilled, low paid jobs. And the goal of workplace equality, especially for women, must be fully realised.

Ian Christie and Ken Worpole set out a vision of a society where improving quality of life, rather than just the standard of living, is the goal of Government. Labour must seriously invest in—and maintain—the social and physical environment. And Labour needs to be fun, to present a sense of *joie de vivre* sorely lacking from the prudent first term.

Finally, Michael Jacobs brings together many of the themes which run through the collection in his defence of ideological narrative. Labour needs to articulate its vision for society, if it is to maintain and strengthen its support and transform the political landscape. He suggests as a narrative the idea that 'government is good'—that the public realm and public services are distinct, giving institutional form to 'community'.

The contributions are by no means exhaustive. Important issues have had to be omitted: for example, we took the decision to focus only on domestic policy. Even in the domestic field, it has not been possible to include all the important issues, and contributors have had to be selective.

Nor are the pieces always consistent with each other; contributors were given a free hand to set out their own views and priorities. However, the thoughts collected here do offer some coherent directions for a more radical second term. Clearly, the importance of equality and the value of the public realm feature prominently. But other themes appear: the need to do more to decentralise, both in terms of the delivery of public services and of political decision-making; seeing through the cultural and institutional changes that will make 'joined-up' government a reality; and, throughout, the desire to see Labour lead public debate with greater confidence and clarity.

G D H Cole, in the 1949 pamphlet, argued that:

> When Let Us Face the Future [the 1945 manifesto] was drawn up, we accepted it as a good, moderate programme, embodying as much … as an energetic Government could be expected to carry through in five years, in face of all the special complexities of the post-war settlement… The first five years, we thought, would have cleared the ground and got the foundations well and truly laid; and in the second term the Government would be able to go full speed ahead.

If Labour is to use its second term to the full, it must make its task nothing short of the transformation of Britain. That is the best possible platform for a third full term.

1 | Social Justice Adrian Harvey

Before the 1997 election, a number of leading Labour spokespeople made it clear that the criterion against which the administration should be judged was its impact on poverty. For many in the Labour Party that was simply a statement of the obvious, albeit a welcome one. Throughout its history, Labour has regarded the pursuit of social justice as a priority, if not an article of faith. Social democratic politics has rested on the idea that citizens should, as a right, be able to meet their basic needs for income, shelter, education, nutrition and health care, and that this is the precondition for genuine equality of opportunity, whereby people are enabled to make the best of themselves.

The new Government's commitment contrasted strongly with what had gone before. During the Conservative administrations of the 1980s and 1990s, poverty increased vastly in depth and scale. The number of people living in poverty trebled between 1979 and 1992 from five million to over 14 million; one in four of the adult population, and a shameful one in three children[1]. More than this, the Government refused to accept that the problem existed, much less that they had a responsibility to deal with it. As late as 1996, Peter Lilley was arguing that poverty did not exist in the UK.

The change in 1997, therefore, was remarkable. Poverty was 'rediscovered' not only as a legitimate area of responsibility for

Government, but as its benchmark. A series of major policy initiatives followed, some backed by serious money. Notable amongst these was the New Deal for the Unemployed, which benefited from the £4.5 billion windfall tax on the privatised utilities. There were a plethora of other measures, significant either for their resourcing, their innovation or both. The Sure Start programme offers support to very young children and their parents in deprived areas. The National Strategy for Neighbourhood Renewal sets out new ways of working and new resources to address the deep-seated problems of multiply deprived urban areas. The Working Families Tax Credit and the National Minimum Wage—first proposed by the Fabian Society in 1906—finally put a floor under low pay. The recently announced Children's Tax Credit brings around £10 a week to families and has a very long 'taper', only being phased out for higher rate tax payers. The Government also created a Minister for Public Health, charged with addressing health inequalities, recognising for the first time in two decades that social and economic inequalities are the primary determinants of ill-health.

In addition to these individual programmes and policies, there were a number of institutional and symbolic developments. The Social Exclusion Unit, announced in Labour's first summer, established cross-departmental working and brought in people from outside Whitehall. Reporting directly to the Prime Minister, its task was to respond to particularly intractable problems which fell between departmental and agency boundaries. It also signalled a change in language from poverty to 'exclusion'. The shift was not simply linguistic; the concerns now went beyond material deprivation and, particularly, income (indeed, these were played down) and focused on identifying groups and areas which needed to be brought back into the mainstream. Exclusion was about behaviour as much as basic needs, about disaffection as much as income, and about lack of opportunities as much as about inequalities.

Perhaps the single most significant symbolic development was Tony Blair's commitment to eradicate child poverty. In his Beveridge Lecture to Oxford University in March 1999, the Prime Minister said, 'Our historic aim will be for ours to be the first generation to end child poverty, and it will take a generation. It is a 20-year mission but I believe it can be done.'[2] In some ways, this simply reaffirmed the commitments made by a number of ministers that poverty reduction was to be the yardstick of the Government's success. However, it went beyond that in two ways. First, it held up the vision that poverty could be ended, not simply reduced. More importantly, it established a timetable and (later) a set of measures by which its achievement could be judged. The evidence suggests that over 1 million children were lifted out of poverty during the first term and even the Child Poverty Action Group—which does not give praise lightly—cautiously predict that progress towards the long term target is comfortably on track.

Yet despite this evident commitment and activity, the first term was not all good news. There have been set backs and developments which have perplexed and frustrated many outside government. Early in the administration, the Government carried through cuts to Income Support for lone parents which 'lost the Government the support of almost the whole of the informed social policy constituency.'[3] Similarly, the failure to re-introduce adequate cash benefits for asylum seekers—removed in 1996 by the then Conservative Government—remains one of the most unjust actions of Labour's first term.

More generally, the emphasis on 'work for those who can' often gave the impression that 'security for those who can't' was less of a priority. What is more, for those of working age unable—for whatever reason—to find appropriate work, the implications were clear. Not only was their security not to be prioritised—

certainly their incomes were left to stagnate further—but there was an insinuation that they could be regarded as being responsible for their own poverty, perpetuating the distinction between the deserving and undeserving poor. Disturbingly, there is now a discernible drift towards conditional assistance within the emerging work-focused welfare system, which threatens to undermine the very idea of state support as a right, to this group at least.

There was one other cloud over the first term. In the run up to the election, despite the extensive policy programme, the headlines were of widening inequalities between rich and poor. Some saw this as a mark of failure on the part of the Government in its aim to reduce poverty. However, in reality it reveals an unresolved tension at the heart of Labour's approach to social justice. For many in the Labour movement, including those in Government, reducing inequality is central to a just society. This is reflected in policy, for example by the inclusion of income inequality as a performance indicator on child poverty. For others, however, closing the gap is seen as less important than 'lifting the floor'—improving the standard of living for those at the bottom. Combined with an open and meritocratic society, it is argued, a high social floor will deliver social justice. Widening income inequality is not in itself a problem, so long as it is caused by rapidly rising earnings at the top rather than falling standards of living at the bottom.

'Lifting the floor', is a legitimate piece of first aid. The priority for Labour's first term was, rightly, to improve the living standards of the poorest as quickly as possible. But this cannot be a long term route to social justice. A society characterised by deep inequalities in income and wealth cannot offer equality of opportunity: existing inequalities will tend to be replicated—and, if unchecked, become further entrenched—over time, regardless of other measures to achieve mobility. It is an uncomfortable truth for meritocrats, but in a market economy income buys opportunities.

In any case, the level at which a 'high social floor' is set is linked directly to what happens at the top end of the income distribution[4], and must be adjusted accordingly. There must, at the very least, be some basis on which this level is set in the first instance. At present, unless related to some measure of inequality, this can only be done arbitrarily—as has been the case for most benefits. As well as being generally unsatisfactory in an age of evidence-based policy making, arbitrary thresholds are likely to be eroded in real terms, particularly during periods of retrenchment. That is precisely how poverty grew during the 1980s and 1990s.

There is, however, an alternative approach which does have a more substantial objective grounding, whether as part of an egalitarian or meritocratic strategy. Minimum Income Standards define the income required to maintain good health, provide essential needs and participation in the community for different household types[5]. Typically, Minimum Income Standards cost a basket of goods and services required to achieve a particular standard of living. The aim is not that the resulting 'budget' should translate directly in to entitlement levels in the benefits system—or the National Minimum Wage—as these will also depend on other factors, such as the implications for public expenditure, for work incentives, or competitiveness. Rather, Minimum Income Standards serve as a more rational reference point on which decisions can be based. In its first term, Government ruled out Minimum Income Standards; however, there is a very strong case for adopting the approach in the second, especially if the policy focus remains that of lifting the floor.

Despite these divisions between egalitarians and meritocrats, there was a substantial redistribution of income during the first term. Yet this has not been widely promoted—it did not feature in the list of achievements presented to the electorate in June 2001. This modesty is indicative of a strategic weakness of the first term, one which may yet make itself felt, particularly if there is an economic downturn. It is now a cliché that the Government has taxed by stealth; however, it also pursued social justice by stealth. Certainly, there were some high profile announcements and policies—the Working Families Tax Credit is a good example and seldom out of the list of achievements rehearsed by ministers. However, the Government failed to offer sufficient political leadership on social justice as a defining narrative for 21st century Labour.

In large part, this reflects the peculiar timidity that characterised the Government's first term in general, despite its massive majority and consistent poll lead. The desire not to be seen as the party of the poor, so evident in the opposition years of the mid-1990s continued into government. This had two crucial impacts. First, the lack of leadership left potential allies in all sectors outside—and therefore not contributing to—the anti-poverty strategy. Second, the Government failed to shift the terms of debate about poverty and the poor. True, the idea that poverty exists—even the Tory Party are late converts to the cause—is more widely accepted. But opinion polling shows that most people still think that the unemployed get generous benefits and are wilfully idle. This view was not challenged.

There is a danger here. Not only did the Government fail to mobilise others in the task of combating poverty; it also risked undermining the sustainability of the anti-poverty strategy. There is evidence from Ireland that, when unemployment fell sharply in the late 1990s, public hostility to the residual poor increased, making the national anti-poverty strategy more difficult to sustain electorally. Delivering social justice by stealth may have been justified in a cautious first term. But creating a socially just Britain that is sustainable requires more than simply discreetly manipulating the mechanisms of government; it requires a seismic shift in the terms of debate, in civil society, as well as the institutions of government. Achieving that will take longer than a second term. Nevertheless, unless the task is begun now, it is unlikely to be achieved; winning a further mandate to continue the work will be impossible unless the argument has been won.

Building on the success of the first term—and addressing some of its failures—requires action in a number of areas. Here, I want to focus on three: equality; 'mainstreaming' social justice; and political leadership.

On the question of inequality, I have already argued that it does matter what happens at the top as well as the bottom. If the poorest are left behind, albeit with an absolute improvement in living standards, there will not be an inclusive society in which all can achieve their potential. Countries that are more equal are healthier, are happier with themselves and tend to be characterised by greater social mobility. Income inequality is not the only issue, but it is important. As a consequence, there needs to be a move towards more progressive taxation. There has been progress here at the bottom end, notably the 10 per cent starting rate of income tax and the reduction in VAT on fuel. However, at the top end change has been minimal.

The recommendation of the Fabian Society's Commission on Citizenship and Taxation proposed a 50 per cent rate of income tax be levied on taxable income over £100,000. However, during the 2001 election campaign, Labour repeated its pledge not to raise income tax rates. Not only does this almost certainly rule this out; it also makes increases in less progressive indirect taxes more likely. There are other adjustments which could be made—for example around National Insurance or Inheritance Tax—to make the system more progressive. However, in any case, the

Government should start to pave the way for a progressive taxation platform at the next election; unless that is done, the left of centre will be permanently fighting on the ground of the right.

At the bottom end of the income distribution, the obvious priority for the second term is to extend the very welcome increases in some benefits—notably for children and those in work—across the board. Benefits such as Income Support, are up-rated only at the rate of inflation—far outstripped by earnings—and this is one reason why income inequality remains so stubborn. This does not mean that benefits need to be earnings-linked; rather, there should be a step change adjustment to redress the erosion of the last 20 years. This need not be a massive increase. Most people reliant on benefits live within such small margins that even a modest increase would do much to improve both the dignity and security of claimants. The latter is important for a Government concerned with opportunity and social mobility—what the Government may present as opportunities, such as taking part time work, often feel like risks to the insecure and consequently are resisted.

The Government rightly says that the aim should be to lift as many people off benefit as possible, but there will always be those who depend on them at some stage, including during their working age. In a just society, this safety net should at least afford those who need it with the means to meet their basic needs—including, it should be noted, those who have come to the UK seeking asylum.

A related issue is the continued expansion of means testing, which now encompasses many more people, not least as a result of the generosity of the Minimum Income Guarantee for pensioners and the WFTC. Directing money quickly to the poorest is a wholly legitimate enterprise, particularly when the living standards of the poorest have eroded so dramatically over the previous 20 years. However, means testing is still problematic. First, it creates benefit traps and a relatively disadvantaged group of the 'nearly poor'—those just outside the threshold. Second, it risks undermining the commitment of the middle classes to the welfare system since, increasingly, their relationship with it is to pay for a system used by others. Unless they benefit too, there is little reason for them to continue to give political support to the system and—crucially—to the taxes needed to pay for it. If means testing is to expand further, ways need to be found to secure middle class buy-in, as well as to minimise the impact of benefit traps. One possible solution is to ensure that means tests have long tapers that extend into the middle class— such as the Children's Tax Credit.

The Government also needs to move on from the 'special measures' approach of the first term. The pilots, pathfinders and zones of the first term were effective in identifying new ways of working. But the time for testing is over. There needs now to be a process for incorporating poverty eradication into all aspects of government. In part, this is a question of generalising the special measures, for example making Sure Start a national programme. But there is also a great deal to do in 'mainstreaming' social justice into the wider 'modernisation' of public services.

Not least, the spread of performance indicators throughout the public sector—and local government in particular—affords both opportunities and threats. As one of the Government's most powerful tools in influencing the focus of activity, it is clear that objectives for which there are no indicators are unlikely to be priorities for overstretched public agencies. The absence, therefore, of indicators for poverty reduction amongst the performance measures introduced through the modernisation programme not only misses an opportunity, but may actually discourage agencies from making social justice a priority.

All local authorities are subject to a set of 'corporate health' indicators, which provide the headline measures for councils' performance. Currently, there are indicators for race and gender equality, and for sustainable development, but none relating directly to social justice. There is then, a strong case for incorporating anti-poverty performance measures into existing regimes, including corporate indicators and Public Service Agreements, to ensure that the signals from central government emphasise the importance of social justice to core services.

Government should also introduce 'poverty proofing' into policy making in Whitehall. Already adopted in Ireland, this approach formalises an assessment of policy at the design stage for its likely impact on those in poverty. All departments in the Irish Government have adopted it, bringing anti-poverty considerations into the heart of mainstream policy making. Interestingly, the Countryside Agency has recently developed a similar 'rural proofing' mechanism, to ensure that rural issues are not forgotten in policy making, and this has been welcomed by Government.

'Mainstreaming' is not just an issue for Government of course. Especially for those companies providing essential services, including the utilities, food, transport, communications and basic financial services, there is scope for exploring the potential for extending a minimum service standards approach. Such an approach could ensure that, where provided by the private sector, basic services would be accessible to all. This could be achieved through persuasion—as in the case of the basic bank account, which is being introduced to reduce financial exclusion—or legislation—as was the case with the Water Industries Act 1999, which removed the right of water companies to disconnect supplies as a sanction against non-payment.

If Government is to bring the private sector—and others—into the anti-poverty strategy, greater political leadership is essential. Coalition building of this sort requires clear vision and direction. But there also need to be mechanisms to facilitate this, and to create a sense of ownership over the strategy from all parties. By creating a national forum where organisations from all sectors, including representatives of the poor and excluded, could be brought together, the Government would be able both to draw on the resources and expertise of others and to generate commitment to the goal of social justice. At the very least, the Government should call a poverty 'summit' early in its second term, both to bring these players together, and also as a very public restatement of intent.

The wider public must be included in the coalition. If it is to do this, Government must mind its language. The emphasis on benefit fraud, for example, is unhelpful. Fraud exists and is wrong. However, it accounts for around 2 per cent of the DSS budget. The message sent by the recent TV adverts on fraud or rhetoric about welfare dependency casts a long shadow over all those in poverty, and does little to generate support for tackling exclusion. It also contributes to the high level of underclaiming, especially amongst pensioners, as well as the widespread misperception by taxpayers that DSS spending largely featherbeds the work-shy, which is turn undermines support for public spending. It is damaging to vulnerable individuals and to the prospects for a just society.

Labour made some vital inroads into reversing the inequalities and deprivations faced by millions as a result of two decades of neglect, but has still not made social justice the defining narrative of its project. The opportunity is there to make the change from a Britain where 'the poor are always with us' to one where all can meet their basic needs and have genuine opportunities to fulfil their potential. However, if the Government is serious about ending poverty and creating a just society, then it has to show some courage and actively set about winning the widest possible support for that project.

References

1   *Poverty—the facts*, CPAG 1996

2   *Ending Child Poverty—Popular welfare for the 21st century*, Robert Walker (ed), The Policy Press 1999.

3   Jonathan Bradshaw, *Child poverty under Labour*, in *An End in Sight—Tackling child poverty in the UK*, Geoff Fimister (ed), CPAG 2001.

4   The only valid concept of poverty is a relative concept. Ideas of absolute poverty—that is subsistence—are themselves historically and culturally specific, dependent on the norms and extremes of a given society. It is simply not possible to live in the urban West without mains power, whereas in rural Africa—where solid fuels could realistically be collected directly from the environment—mains power can be regarded as non-essential. As the general living standards of a society escalate, so too do the basic needs to subsist within it, as the Government's concern about the 'digital divide' illustrates.

5   Catherine Howarth, Peter Kenway and Guy Palmer, *Responsibility for all—A national strategy for social inclusion*, Fabian Society/New Policy Institute 2001.

"

2| **Public Services** Sue Richards

In May 1997, many people felt exhilarated at the prospect of a new approach to public services; today, there is an emerging consensus that the government of 1997-2001 significantly under-performed in this area. The picture is mixed—there are success areas—but overall the judgement must be one of disappointment. Some of the disappointment is inevitably linked to the spending levels adopted in the first two years, with public expenditure falling to less than 40 per cent of GDP, the Thatcherite Holy Grail. As the Institute of Fiscal Studies recently pointed out, public expenditure as a proportion of GDP has reached a long-term low.

Whilst much attention has been focussed on levels of public spending, there are equally important questions about the policy and programme frameworks through which the money is used. The espoused focus of public policy is on the achievement of outcomes, and this is a welcome development. But in practice, deeply embedded norms of behaviour in the inherited systems combined with ministerial desire to be seen to be doing something fast have reinforced the existing drive towards outputs and militated against the achievement of the outcomes which ministers say they want to achieve. There is something fundamentally misconceived about the basic recipe for change employed.

There are three possible lines of development for the second term. The first is that the same recipe will be continued, or even reinforced, in the future, on the assumption that since we have tried hard, and not succeeded, we need to try doing the same things even harder. A second possibility has been aired in the manifesto—we have tried hard, and it has not worked, so we will bring in the cavalry from the private sector. Finally, it is just possible that ministers will recognise that public service change comes through a steady process of development rather than the 'heroic' 60 yard dash, and settle down to achieving it.

The incoming Labour Government in 1997 recognised that successful intervention into deep-seated social problems like low skills, fear of crime and inequalities in health was a key part of delivering a third way programme. This involved continuing the search for global competitiveness pursued by the previous regime, but also undertaking successful supply side interventions to overcome the multiple and interlocking problems of social exclusion.

Such a change sounds like a small step, but actually it is a giant leap. It involves managing a balance between two competing approaches—European social democracy and American capitalism—each of which has its own logic and symmetry. But, in combination, these logics fight each other, always in danger of reverting to one type or the other. In order to make the successful supply side interventions, fundamental change in the structures, systems, processes and competences of the public policy system was needed, but at the same time the competence developed in cutting costs and efficient management must be maintained and cherished.

The 1997 Government inherited a culture of cost containment, emphasising the ratio between inputs and outputs. This had become deeply embedded over the Thatcher and Major years, and it permeated all parts of the public sector, particularly Whitehall. This 'more for less' paradigm had involved central-

ising power, reducing the autonomy of public service profes-
sionals—in order to deliver the strategy—reducing taxation to
free up the entrepreneurial side of the economy, and injecting
market forces and the disciplines of competition into public
service provision.

The application of this model over twenty years naturally left
its mark. Managerial capacity had been developed, in both
people and processes. Professional practice had become more
transparent and accountable. Performance measurement got
better, although mainly the measurement of outputs rather than
outcomes. The new Labour Government took on this inheritance.
It was faced with the challenge of trying to move beyond the
output-driven paradigm and graft on the capacity to achieve
effective outcomes, but failed fully to address the re-design
issues involved. The essence of the problem is that outputs had
been designed primarily to reduce unit costs, and were measured
within existing structures of accountability. Outcomes are real-
world changes which are no respecters of organisational boundaries.

A diagnostic narrative had developed before the election about
the changes which would be necessary to deliver the new
Government's strategy. The 'wicked' problems were key—problems which eluded solution because they fell between the silo
structures, the policy domains sponsored by different Whitehall
departments and mirrored in localities. Only if government
could work in a more 'joined-up' way, it was argued, would it
stand a chance of solving these problems.

This work was taken forward positively in government in a
number of ways. Two units at the centre of Whitehall were very
significant—the Social Exclusion Unit and the Performance and
Innovation Unit. The key contribution of the former was the
development of the National Strategy for Neighbourhood
Renewal and, of the latter, two reports—Wiring it up and

Reaching Out—which diagnosed key design problems in the system of government. These reports form the basis of a plan for developing an outcomes-driven public policy system, but have not really been taken into the heart of government strategy. It took four years to develop the neighbourhood renewal action plan, for instance, and many of the proposals in the two PIU reports remain unimplemented. Meanwhile, instead of change happening in a coherent and strategic way, we saw each Whitehall department spawning its own local action zones, which soon became part of the problem of fragmentation rather than part of the joining-up solution.

The greatest process innovation on joined-up government has come from the Treasury, which has so come to dominate social policy during this period of government. The key instruments have been two rounds of fundamental review—the Comprehensive Spending Review of 1998 and the Spending Review of 2000. There have been fundamental reviews before, but these were not undertaken with an explicit remit to set out desirable outcomes, and then redraw public sector structure and process better to achieve them.

Two specific results of the first review made major contributions to developing an outcome focus. Following a study of public provision for children under 8, proposals for the Sure Start programme were set out. They were outcome-focused, evidence-based and given an appropriate governance and accountability framework, with cross-departmental ministerial responsibility and a performance system based on outcomes, evaluation and learning, rather than outputs specified from the centre. The other success story was the review of the criminal justice system, which set out overarching strategic aims and outcomes which united the two main criminal justice departments (together with the Crown Prosecution Service), creating partnership structures and processes to enable criminal justice to be a 'system'.

Reviews do not necessarily result in real world change, but here they were linked with another innovation, Public Service Agreements. These were constructed as contract-like agreements between the Treasury and spending departments, setting out the outcomes to be delivered in exchange for the public expenditure allocated. Actually, in the first PSAs there were probably more targets for outputs than outcomes, but there was an aspiration to be outcome-focused which was realised more fully in the second round in 2000.

The story so far is of the good news. Unfortunately, that is not the whole picture. Alongside the new focus on outcomes there was a continuation of the older focus on outputs, with no clear evidence that contradictions between the two were recognised or handled. The explanation for this may be found in the following statement from a member of the No 10 Policy Unit, in a seminar held shortly after the 1997 election: 'I used to think we should be tight on the ends to be achieved, but loose on the means. Now I think we should be tight on both'.

This illustrates the immensely seductive notion that once you have your hands on power, all you need to do to make things happen is to pull a lever and five million public servants will start delivering. It also suggests that the man or woman in Whitehall, temporary or permanent, knows better than people in the field how to achieve the objectives. In an output-driven para-digm, this would be true, since people on the front line would not have the same incentive to reduce unit costs as those in the centre. After all, it would mean losing their jobs or increasing their workload. But achieving outcomes on these complex social problems requires both the right central strategy and also the capacity to make differentiated judgements about complex local circumstances, and cannot be achieved without incorporating that local judgement.

The key role of the centre is not to be tight on the means of delivery, but to build the capacity of local deliverers to handle their task well. However, there are many examples of local capacity being squandered or central directives which fly in the face of local knowledge about what works. Here are just a few examples.

Primary Care Groups have been established on too small a population base, resulting in insufficient capacity to carry out their role of commissioning services. Failure to learn from well-established knowledge has necessitated mergers and other structural change as PCGs become trusts, contributing to the long NHS tradition of continuous structural change which has so damaged its capacity to perform. Additionally, despite a Cabinet decision to go for alignment of boundaries between local bodies to facilitate partnership working, this was not done in the case of PCGs and has led to reduced capacity for local partnership. Other local agencies throw up their hands in despair at the health sector.

In education, there are many positive achievements, some of them through centralisation, as in the case of the numeracy and literacy hours which seem to be paying off in overall results, bringing poor performers up to the average and only temporarily suppressing the innovation of the best. Policies for improved standards can only be achieved by improving the capacity to deliver. The government has rightly focused on developing the leadership capacities of head teachers, but scored a massive own goal in its continued cherishing of a chief inspector of schools who had ceased to have a useful role in improving standards. His personal style may have been necessary to get change on the agenda back in the early 1990s, but for the life of the first new labour government it was an obstacle to improving standards, and has provided the next government with its biggest education problem, teacher shortage. It requires mature strategic judgement to know where to draw the line between the destructive phase of a change programme, designed to unfreeze an under-performing culture, and the constructive phase of building the capacity to perform. This judgement has not prevailed, and the Chief Inspector has been allowed to serve his own agenda. Thankfully at last, Ofsted has embarked on a much more appropriate style of operation.

In criminal justice, the police were provided with powers to impose local area curfews for children of 10 or under who are out unsupervised at night. The purpose was to bring about a reduction in anti-social behaviour which was reducing the quality of life for other residents. Some finger-wagging crossness from the Home Office followed the report that none of these curfews had actually been implemented, and pressure was put upon local police forces to do so. This is a nice illustration of the centre believing that it can be 'tight on the means' even when it does not have available the experiential knowledge and capacity for judgement available to those who are closer to the problem. Such people believe that there are better ways of handling the anti-social behaviour of young people, better for them and for the future safety of their community—which is why they did not use curfews.

In local government, a new performance regime designed to promote a culture of self-improvement—Best Value—was hijacked by the creation of a vast set of Best Value Performance Indicators. This was the product of a trawl around Whitehall requesting departments to set out what performance indicators they would like to establish for local government. The result is a performance framework with almost 200 indicators, some measuring outcomes, but most concerned with inputs or outputs. This imposed a flavour of bureaucratic nightmare on the whole programme

What these examples reveal is the desire to bring about substantial change in a limited period. The desired outcomes are to be applauded—a more coherent approach to health commissioning than was previously possible through the mess of GP fundholding, better standards of achievement in schools, safer communities. The mistake was to have an inadequately developed strategy for achieving these outcomes—or if there was a strategy, not ensuring compliance with it or applying it across the board. And linked with a coherently designed strategy needs to be an appropriate plan for leading and managing change.

It is helpful to think of managing change in terms of a menu of techniques and processes, each of which is appropriate to a different change management task. In its publication on managing change, the Audit Commission suggests that there are two dimensions on which change needs to be planned. Change can be either directive or organic, and it can be either step-change or incremental. Putting those two dimensions together gives us a fourfold typology of change, each type suited to particular circumstances, and possibly of utility in the same setting at different stages of the change life cycle:

- directive step change ('surgery' on organisational structures and systems)
- directive incremental change ('operational improvement' in efficiency of processes).
- organic step change ('transformation' of organisational culture)
- organic incremental change (learning and evolution)

Each of these models of change will have its place in the strategy, but the right model must be picked for the right circumstances. What seems to have happened is that the directive step-change model has predominated, even though the purpose of change has rarely been that to which this model is suited, the surgical excision of existing structures and processes.

This model has the superficial attraction of appearing strong and determined, making it particularly appealing to a new set of ministers without very much experience of organisational change. It was reasonably well-suited to a public policy paradigm based on the principles of 'more for less', when questions about outcomes did not count for much. It does have a place in an outcome driven paradigm, and may be the first phase of a change programme, but unless the emphasis migrates to the 'organic' part of the model, whether transformation or evolution, our capacity to achieve outcomes in the area of wicked problems will be reduced rather than enhanced.

Perhaps the most worrying reflection on the talk about involving the private sector more in public services is that this is another onslaught of directive step-change, cutting out public managers and replacing them with private managers who, it is assumed, will be more capable of managing the complex, professionally dominated services through which the public will assess Government's achievements at the next election.

Experience shows us that contracting out manual (easily specified) services can produce big one-off gains in cost and quality. But the greater the information asymmetry between purchaser and provider—where the provider is the only party able to specify the service needed in a particular case—the less gain there is to be made, and the greater the transaction costs in managing the contract. In such circumstances, the employment contract is a better bet than the service contract.

This is the conventional wisdom of transaction cost economics, empirically tested very thoroughly in the 'more for less' paradigm. Attachment to the myth of the private sector as super-hero needs to be qualified by hard facts and tough analysis in the preparation of future strategy to involve the private sector in delivering public services like health and education. A pragmatic approach is essential, considering the nature of the service, the nature of the market, the degree of information asymmetry and the cost of risk management. Without this underpinning policy analysis, disastrous mistakes are possible.

This analysis suggests that there are many good ideas around, but inadequate means for developing a strategy to put them into practice. The success of the Treasury in the creation of Public Service Agreements provides further evidence in support of this point of view. In the public expenditure planning process, the Treasury has the power and authority to bring about a coherent strategy for change. At both ministerial and official level there is a clear view about what needs to be done. Unfortunately, finance is only one of several drivers which need to be brought together to achieve change in outcomes, and in between the spending review processes, other less integrating factors predominate.

The balance of incentives on ministerial behaviour does not appear to be well-matched to the needs of the paradigm. Despite the fact that secretaries of state have enjoyed an unparalleled period of longevity, some ministers still go for short-term wins that damage long-term capacity. Assuming that they are rational individuals, and that they have information about incentives that the rest of us do not have, the conclusion to be drawn is that the agenda of long term capacity building is not being driven firmly from the top, but is in practice being sacrificed in exchange for some quick hits on public opinion.

This may be an appropriate thing to do at this stage of the political game, but in the election of 2005 the government will be judged against the public's real experience of public services and public policy outcomes. To achieve real benefit from the extra money being poured in, so that it actually feels different for service users and front line staff, we need a much more coherently managed programme of change. This must be designed to build capacity and encourage performance.

This is not a soft-hearted, human relations approach, but comes from a hard-headed appreciation of the logic of service management, and the significance of frontline staff in the public's perception of the service. The head of Scandinavian Airlines described 10,000 moments of truth about his organisation every day, each time a customer interacted with a service deliverer. For Tony Blair it is five million moments of truth. The task is to win their support, not try to batter them into submission.

3| **Democracy** Meg Russell

Constitutional reform was probably the biggest achievement of Labour's first term in office. The list of measures enacted in just four years is startling. The right of hereditary peers to sit in the House of Lords was ended after 700 years. A parliament was restored to Scotland, with extensive law making powers. Assemblies were created in Wales and Northern Ireland, with all three new bodies elected by proportional systems that ensured no single party won overall control. A proportional system of voting was also introduced for the election of the UK's MEPs. London regained its own Assembly and, for the first time, got a directly elected mayor. Legislation changing executive structures in local government was passed, with more elected mayors on the way in other towns and cities. Regional Development Agencies were established in the eight English regions outside London, and each is now coupled with an indirectly elected regional chamber. The Human Rights Act gave UK citizens access to European Convention rights for the first time through domestic courts, and is feeding through into policy processes in Whitehall and Westminster. These institutions will also be influenced by the new Freedom of Information Act. There were changes to the regulation of political parties and referendums, with the establishment of a new Electoral Commission and stricter spending rules. Finally, voting experiments led to an opening up of postal voting and reform of electoral registration.

Despite two unfulfilled manifesto commitments in the constitutional field, the government can hardly be accused of inaction during its first term. The programme of reform has been ambitious by any standard and the changes will have profound effects. The criticism which Labour has suffered is rather that this was not a 'programme' at all, so much as a collection of piecemeal actions which do not add up to a whole. The task for the future must therefore be to create a coherence in Labour's approach, with any further reforms used to bind the previous changes together rather than risk further accusations of fragmentation. This must be the priority for a Labour second term.

In creating coherence there are three related questions which must be asked. First, what is the underlying rationale behind the reform programme: what is its objective? Second, how can the individual reforms be best made to fit together? And third, how can the administration of the programme itself be made coherent and consistent in terms, for example, of responsibilities within Whitehall and of the timing of different reforms?

One of the difficulties is that the first of these has rarely been spelled out clearly. The last time this was done substantially was in a Labour Party policy statement in 1993[1]. This mentioned three related principles underlying the desire for constitutional reform. The first was a desire to strengthen the 'checks and balances' in the system and guard against untrammelled executive power. The second, to introduce greater 'pluralism', reflected a desire to move from away from Britain's 'majoritarian' tradition and towards a 'consensus' model of decision making. The third was to 'decentralise' policy making, whilst stopping short of advocating a fully federal model. These principles provided a clear basis on which to build individual reforms. However, in subsequent statements it was primarily these reforms, and more generalised statements of intent (such as 'creating a new relationship between the citizen and the state' and 'an open, responsive democracy') which have dominated. If the objective of the second term is to draw together the reforms which have taken place and provide coherence, this is the time to return to the principles underlying the programme and review how they are best achieved.

There are three main pieces of unfinished business which the government will be under pressure to action in its second term: House of Lords reform, electoral reform for the House of Commons and creation of elected assemblies in the English regions[2]. All were promised in the 1997 manifesto, but none have yet come fully to fruition. All three were again included in the 2001 manifesto. The question is whether these reforms be used to bind the constitutional settlement together in the second term.

House of Lords reform is only partially complete. A bill passed in 1999 removed most of the hereditary peers (although some remain as a result of the 'Weatherill compromise'). But this ended only the most obvious anachronism. Further reform of the chamber was given a longer timescale, with a Royal Commission, chaired by Conservative Lord Wakeham, established to consider the options. It was faced with a huge task: to make proposals on the 'role and functions' of the upper house as well as its composition. This involved considering the legislative and investigative powers of the chamber, the mix of elected and appointed members who might sit in it, and how they would be chosen. But the Commission was also required to address diverse issues such as the role of the Law Lords and of religious representatives in the house. And it was explicitly—and rightly—asked to consider how a reformed chamber might fit with other aspects of constitutional reform such as devolution and the new human rights framework.

The Commission's report in January 2000 was not met with a

positive response, and its publication felt like the beginning rather than the end of the debate. Lord Wakeham had attempted to deliver a solution which would be acceptable to the government, but found few other takers for his largely appointed chamber, in which a minority of elected members would represent the nations and regions, and religious and judicial representation would be retained. The government wished to proceed by consensus with the other parties, but no such agreement could be reached. The proposed parliamentary committee to examine the next stage of reform was thus never established, and even the bipartisan talks with the Liberal Democrats broke down early in 2001. The 2001 manifesto expresses support for Wakeham, although the prominence given to 'removal of the remaining hereditary peers' raises concerns that Government could try to pursue this objective alone, leaving the chamber otherwise exactly as it is.

On electoral reform for the Commons, the Jenkins report was shelved because of intra rather than inter party disagreement. This Commission reported in October 1998, proposing the 'alternative vote plus' system, whereby 80-85 per cent of MPs would be elected in single member constituencies and the remainder from party lists. Outcomes under this system would not be as proportional as many electoral reformers would have wished, but were accepted by most as a necessary compromise. However, defenders of the status quo within the Labour Party fought hard to put the proposals on hold and the promised referendum on the voting system was not held during the first term. The 2001 manifesto renewed the commitment to reform, but stated that the effects of the mixed-member systems for the Scottish Parliament and National Assembly for Wales would be further assessed.

On devolution in England the 1997 manifesto had promised 'in time' to 'introduce legislation to allow the people, region by region, to decide in a referendum whether they want directly elected regional government'. There was no such legislation and no referendums were held, although campaigns for elected assemblies are now established in several of the regions. Five regions have constitutional conventions, based on the successful Scottish model, two of which are drawing up detailed plans. Others—notably the South East and Eastern regions—have shown little enthusiasm yet. The 2001 manifesto restated the earlier commitment.

Apart from these major issues which the government knows it needs to address, and has formulated policy on, there are others where they will be pressured to act but will be less enthusiastic. One is further devolution in Wales, where there is frustration at the current arrangements. The Assembly has no primary legislative powers and is thus forced to lobby Westminster for parliamentary time. A commission in Wales will make proposals on the Assembly's powers after the 2003 elections and may propose a settlement closer to that in Scotland. In assessing these claims, and the claims of the English regions, the government needs to decide how far it is prepared to travel along the decentralisation path. More immediate pressure will face the government on the 'modernisation' of the House of Commons, where changes implemented in the first term were minor, despite initial high hopes. Opposition parties, various independent groups, commissions, and parliamentary committees, have produced a wealth of proposals to both strengthen parliament and make it more hospitable for members. The first of these objectives is important to keeping the government accountable and the second to improving the representative nature of parliament. If pluralism and checks and balances remain among Labour's objectives, the new government would want to respond positively to these demands.

The issues of electoral reform, Lords reform, devolution and reform of the Commons are far from disconnected. Indeed parliament remains the central structure of government, but remains largely unreformed. The government's attitude to parliamentary reform will be important in the success of attempts to introduce coherence.

One issue on which the government is facing pressure from the opposition but where it is reluctant to act is the impact of devolution on the House of Commons. The Conservatives, with no representation in Westminster from Scotland or Wales from 1997-2001, became increasingly concerned about the so-called 'West Lothian Question'. This asks how Scottish members can be allowed to vote on matters for England, such as health and education, which are devolved to the Parliament in Scotland. With a big Labour majority in England this is a largely academic question, since government does not rely on the support of Scottish MPs. But a Labour government with a small majority could, in theory, use the votes of Scots to impose its policy on England. Thus 'English votes on English laws' became a central pledge within the Conservatives' proposals for parliamentary reform. Such a solution has also been proposed by Frank Field and, in a weaker form, by the Procedure Committee of the House of Commons.

The West Lothian Question is an issue for two reasons, both of which may potentially be resolved, at least in part, by progress on the issues Labour has promised to advance. Primarily, the question arises because of the asymmetry of the current devolution settlement. Matters which Scottish MPs used to raise in the House of Commons are now devolved to the Scottish Parliament, whilst responsibility for the same issues in England continues to rest at Westminster. The lack of elected English regional assemblies (or an English Parliament) makes this contrast particularly stark. Thus, many reformers see the solution lying in accelerating devolution in England. This is unlikely to provide the whole answer, since assemblies will not have Scottish-type powers in the foreseeable future. However, it would ease the pressure. If Labour's vision includes a gradual progress towards a more symmetrical federal solution (where Wales catches up with Scotland and is followed in time by some English regions) the problem would eventually dissolve. This was the way devolution in Spain developed in the 1980s, where the 'West Barcelona Question' never arose.

The second factor aggravating the question is the electoral system (notably different here to in Spain). The problem is exacerbated because Labour is overrepresented in Scotland as compared to England, and this is in part because of first past the post. Labour is more popular in Scotland than in England, for example gaining 46 per cent of Scottish votes and 44 per cent of English votes in 1997. However, this is exaggerated in the distribution of seats, where Labour held 78 per cent of Scottish seats and 62 per cent of English seats after that election. A more proportional distribution of seats to votes would therefore help to end this anomaly. Added to devolution in England, and the planned reduction of Scottish seats in the Commons at the next boundary review, it would much reduce the likelihood of particular controversies over the exercise of Scottish votes in the Commons. This is one example, therefore, of where further constitutional reform might be used to tie up loose ends from the first term, and make the settlement more coherent. If further decentralisation and changes to the voting system are Labour's objectives, then our current position may be seen as only a staging post.

However, the party's position is more ambivalent than that, with neither English devolution nor electoral reform for the Commons likely to be delivered in full by the government in its second term. The Jenkins proposals were for only a semi-proportional electoral system, and even this may be difficult to deliver before the next general election[3]. By 2005 there may be elected regional assemblies in some areas—most likely the North East and North West—but in other areas there is little appetite yet for this reform. On top of this there remain some arguments about regional boundaries—for example in the South West where the Cornish have established their own constitutional convention. And local government reform introduces a further complication, with many predicting conflict between the establishment of elected mayors in major cities and of region-wide governance.

Add House of Lords reform to the picture and it becomes more complex and potentially contradictory. In many countries the upper house is used to tie the constitution together, both through its design and through its functions. In federal or devolved countries it will tend to comprise representatives of the regions, provinces or states and it may also have a veto over constitutional reform. Using this kind of territorial representation answers the question of how to have two distinct chambers constituted differently. Hence the Wakeham commission was asked to consider how House of Lords reform might link to devolution.

The model they proposed, essentially, was a halfway house between the federal model and the upper chamber we currently have. The chamber would be charged with acting as 'a voice for the nations and regions', although only a minority of members would be elected territorially, with the remainder appointed from the centre. It would therefore be given a linking role post-devolution but would most likely be unable to fulfil it. Alongside this hybrid house would remain the House of Commons, whose members all have a geographical connection to their constituencies. Already the Commons has territorial committees for Scotland, Wales and Northern Ireland (which were not disbanded post-devolution as some had anticipated) and party groups which organise along regional boundaries. A committee for the English regions was recently established. The Commons therefore has a head start in being able to forge links to the new Assemblies and Parliament (though it has yet to do much in practice). It is difficult to see how an upper house which was only weakly territorial could compete—with a resulting lack of clarity about the links between Westminster and the devolved institutions. Thus further reform, unless carefully planned, could serve to confuse rather than cement the new constitutional arrangements.

These difficulties lead to the conclusion that a greater proportion of upper house members should have strong regional links, and therefore that a greater proportion should probably be elected[4]. But thinking about the mix of elected and appointed members in the chamber leads also into questions about the extent to which the executive should be checked, and through which parts of the system greater plurality should be provided. This presents a potential conflict between Lords reform and reform of the voting system for the House of Commons.

Many of those dissatisfied with Wakeham's report—including the Liberal Democrats, SNP, Plaid Cymru and some in the Labour Party—argue for a chamber which is fully elected by a proportional system. This would have the advantage of giving greater legitimacy to the upper house whilst strengthening its regional links. Amongst these groups, and campaigners such as Charter88, demands for PR for the Commons and a reformed upper house both aim to strengthen parliament and introduce plurality into the system. However, whilst a proportionally elected lower house and upper house may be individually attractive, put together they do not make sense. It is well established that the many benefits of two-chamber parliaments are lost unless the two chambers bring different perspectives to bear. Today this largely depends on different electoral majorities.

A proportional upper house alongside the current House of Commons is logical, but alongside a proportionally elected

Commons it would add nothing distinctive. Putting it another way, a mixed elected-appointed chamber alongside the current House of Commons does little to strengthen parliament, but alongside a more proportional House of Commons it could make sense (provided, I would personally suggest, that the elected regional element comprised at least 50 per cent). Commons and Lords reform must therefore be progressed together, as distinct elements in a coherent constitutional package.

In the absence of clear underlying principles, there is a danger that future reforms will be carried out piecemeal, and not bring the consistency which is needed. Here, both government and campaigners suffer from the fragmented structure within Whitehall, which makes it difficult to take a more coherent approach. This is the third way in which consistency needs to be introduced[5]. In the first term responsibility for constitutional reform was scattered within Whitehall, with the Home Office responsible for electoral reform and human rights, the Cabinet Office for Lords reform, and the DETR for English devolution. There were also the three territorial ministries for Scotland, Wales and Northern Ireland—although these may be rationalised after the election. The Lord Chancellor's Department (where Derry Irvine took an interest in the programme as a whole) was responsible for the judiciary.

These arrangements made strategic thinking difficult, even with the addition of a cabinet committee on Constitutional Reform. The risk is that they will prevent it in the crucial second term. The Constitution Unit has long argued for a minister who acts as 'constitutional reform supremo' to provide coherence and strategic thinking, and the importance of this function is perhaps greater now than ever. Without a stronger centre there is a danger that the constitutional settlement will not be given the coherence that it needs.

It falls to government to set out the vision of where they are trying to take us, and a stronger centre seems essential to achieving that. Given the recent lack of debate over the big picture, public consultation is also key. Through such an exercise, which might take the form of a White Paper, a Royal Commission, or even a full-blown constitutional convention, both outside groups and government would also be forced to take a more holistic perspective and address the potential conflicts between their various favoured reforms. This could provide an opportunity for compromise between the supporters of majoritarianism and consensus politics both within and outside the Labour Party, and lead to a more settled view. Whilst reform in the first term was far-reaching, we have got this far in typical British fashion, through piecemeal and gradualist change. In the second term government must grasp the nettle of where exactly it wants the constitution to go.

References

1   *A New Agenda for Democracy*

2   I exclude from this discussion the possible adoption of the Euro, which would have important constitutional consequences.

3   See R Hazell, *Unfinished Business: Implementing Labour's Constitutional Agenda for a Second Term*, Constitution Unit 2001, for a discussion of why this is the case.

4   For a discussion of how regional links to the upper house might be strengthened see M Russell, *Reforming the House of Lords: Lessons from Overseas*, Oxford University Press 2000.

5   When considering implementation, there are also some difficult timing issues—discussed in R Hazell, *op cit.*

4| **Economy** Jonathan Michie

L abour enjoyed a relatively easy ride on the economy over its first term. Not least, it inherited fast growth, which remained sufficient for employment to continue rising and unemployment falling. The second term, however, may prove trickier.

The main macro-economic questions hinge on two factors that Gordon Brown may be able to influence, but to some extent are out of his hands—whether the world economy slides into recession, and whether Tony Blair calls a referendum on the Euro. One economic factor that remains firmly in the hands of the Chancellor, though, is taxation.

In the first term, the Treasury's task has been to deliver increased public spending, lower taxes and reduced borrowing. They largely achieved this through a combination of good fortune and stealth. Although Labour had made various promises requiring public spending—and hence taxation—the commitment to stick to the Tories' spending plans let the Chancellor off this particular hook for the first two years. Alongside this, the economic growth inherited from Kenneth Clarke's low interest rate regime provided healthy taxation revenues. And the combination of these, along with windfalls from higher oil prices and hence tax revenues plus the mobile phone auction, allowed budget surpluses to reduce the national debt[1].

There were, though, a number of worrying developments on taxation. First there was a switch from progressive direct taxation to regressive indirect taxation. This switch contributed to increased inequality during the Government's first term, with the proportion of income paid in tax falling for the richest 20 per cent of households since 1997-8 but rising for the bottom 80 per cent. Someone in the poorest fifth of households now pays on average 41 per cent of their overall income on tax compared to 36 per cent for the richest fifth.

Coupled with this, the expansion of means testing has resulted—ironically, given the low tax rhetoric—in extremely high marginal tax rates for the least well off as benefits get withdrawn following any rise in earnings. This shift away from universal benefits also threatens to undermine the political and social support for the welfare state, changing it from being a collective enterprise to which all contribute and from which all benefit, to a large charity giving exercise. This combination of moving to regressive indirect taxation and means testing benefits has resulted in tax rates—both marginal and average—being higher for the least well off than they are for the rich. Reversing this should be the Chancellor's top priority.

Labour opened its first term by handing interest rate policy to the Bank of England's Monetary Policy Committee. The rationale was that this would avoid sterling being forced down by international currency markets suspicious of a Labour Government. The result has been that the currency has been overvalued instead, damaging the traded goods sector, most dramatically with BMW abandoning Rover and Corus closing steel plants.

Such problems would be considerably amplified if the UK were to join the Euro as currently constituted. The danger is that, within the single currency, the economy may become tied to inappropriate interest rates and/or exchange rates. Recent events have demonstrated that the European Central Bank makes interest rate decisions according to the economic needs of Germany rather than Ireland. If the Euro were to become over-valued against the dollar in the future, this would be less of a problem for other European economies than for the UK. In this situation, the danger would be that the European Central Bank might allow such a state of affairs to continue rather than cut interest rates.

Either of these possibilities—of the Euro resulting in either an inappropriate interest rate or exchange rate for the UK economy—could prove disastrous economically, socially and politically. The key aim of the Labour Government—well before any consideration of whether or not to join the single currency is made—should therefore be to bring about change in the nature of European Monetary Union. In particular, it is vital to democratise the institutions and functioning of the single currency, and to challenge the orthodox, deflationary logic that has driven the single currency process to date. The so called Stability and Growth Pact, under which the Irish Government was recently reprimanded for planning tax cuts, despite having a large budget surplus, should be abandoned. Indeed, the same meeting of European Finance Ministers that reprimanded Ireland also warned that Gordon Brown's taxation plans might fail their test.

An area which has featured prominently in Gordon Brown's thinking is that of productivity and innovation. There is certainly plenty of work for the second term—much of it requiring action not only from the Treasury but also from the DTI and other Departments.

On productivity, the first term was largely a wasted term. However, one measure that Gordon Brown did take was to give tax incentives to employee shareholder trusts to encourage greater commitment from workers to the organizations for which they work, thus hoping to boost productivity. The recognition that the way to improve economic performance is to invest in the workforce is to be welcomed. It is in marked contrast to the previous Conservative administrations that regarded the work force as the problem for British industry rather than as part of the solution.

Successive labour market deregulation and anti-trade union legislation aimed to create a flexible 'hire-and-fire' labour market. All the evidence shows that this is a low road to nowhere. Firms that took this route during the 1980s proved to be less innovative, not more. In some cases there was a positive effect on the short-term financial performance of these firms, but invariably there was a negative effect on labour productivity and product quality. Short-term financial gain may explain the use by some employers of these types of flexible work practices, particularly if under short-term financial pressure. But the gains that the companies make in short-term profitability are not generated from improved productivity. Rather they represent a shift from wages to profits. While it is understandable for firms to resort to such practices, succumbing to such temptation represents ultimately a self-defeating short-termism to the detriment of productivity and product quality on which the firm's financial success itself is ultimately dependent.

Workplaces with trade unions, on the other hand, proved more likely to invest in research and development and new products. The best performing companies were those that turned their backs on the deregulated labour market of short-term, temporary contracts and the like and instead invested in progressive human resource practices, including employment guarantees and employee involvement[2].

Labour needs to build on the 2000 budget moves on employee shareholder trusts (on which, see below), to commit decisively to the high road option of employee involvement and commitment, innovation and productivity growth. The low road option of a deregulated labour market needs to be discarded.

On innovation, investment in 'high commitment work systems', including employment guarantees, has also been shown to play an important role. In addition, there have been welcome moves to integrate innovation, industrial and regional policies, and Lord Sainsbury has been encouraging the development of Regional Innovation Strategies. It is important that these policies be co-ordinated for all regions, but particularly in order to tackle the 'regional innovation paradox'. Those areas most in need of investment in innovation are precisely those least able firstly to attract the necessary funds and secondly to then absorb and utilise such investments productively[3].

It is also vital that Regional Innovation Strategies network effectively to not just spread best practice but to develop best practice. The DTI has acknowledged the need for such networking and at the time of writing appears to be working to establish it. This is an area where the Labour Government could deliver in a significant and uncontroversial area relatively easily and cheaply. But it needs to go beyond bland generalisations about supporting innovation, to taking action that actually changes the way that companies behave—causing them to invest, innovate and grow in ways they otherwise would not.

Industrial policy has sometimes been derided as an attempt by bureaucrats to 'pick winners', when this is best left to the market. The problem of course is that the 'market' will not necessarily pick winners. Many healthy firms are killed off unnecessarily by market forces. Many more potential winners never see the light of day. Perhaps because the necessary start up investment was not available—at least not on the right terms or in the right form. There may have been just too many uncertainties over the prospects for market growth, over the availability of suitably skilled labour, or some other factor. This is where the Government needs to be intervening. Not necessarily to 'pick winners', but to create winners that otherwise will not come into existence at all, or at least will not succeed in achieving what they might.

There has been a long-standing public debate and considerable literature on the problems of short-termism in British industry, on whether UK firms are starved of investment funds by the City. There is no doubt that small innovative companies do find it hard to attract long-term start up funding from the City. Ridiculously short payback times are expected. The rates of return demanded may be fine for speculators but not for those wanting to develop new products or services over a period of years. Even where funds are made available, too often these are of a short-term nature, sometimes even in the form of overdraft facilities repayable on demand. A demand for immediate repayment will usually bankrupt the company. So there is a need for patient long-term start up and development funding for firms.

In addition to appropriate funding, there are important benefits to firms of being part of a successful cluster of economic activity, and this is something that regional innovation strategies can assist with. Potentially this can allow expensive infrastructure to be shared by firms, if necessary being provided by the public sector. It can assist in supporting R&D and training, where there are common requirements across the cluster of firms. There is scope for the public sector to not just co-ordinate activity but to provide common facilities and services that require economies of scale.

The UK still rates poorly in international comparisons of civil R&D expenditure[4], training and other key factors for successful innovation and industrial growth. Improving performance in these areas needs to be an explicit policy aim for the second term.

Before the 1997 election, there was much talk of 'stakeholding'. Successive governments have recognized the problem of poor corporate governance in the UK, but there were hopes that an incoming Labour Government would act to ensure that companies' boards of directors would take proper account of the interests of all stakeholders. Again, the first term missed the chance to make important improvements to the functioning of the economy fairly easily and—the all-important criteria—costlessly.

The Company Law Review report is not yet published, but it is expected to be disappointing for those hoping to see clear leadership on corporate governance. The existing Combined Code on corporate governance is widely ignored by companies[5]; it needs to be given statutory force. Consumers, employees and the public sector should all be encouraged to participate in the corporate governance of firms. This includes a presence in the boardroom through directors elected by consumer and employee shareholder trusts and, where appropriate, with public interest directors appointed by local, regional or national government.

Government could also democratise the employee shareholder trusts now being established following Gordon Brown's 2000 budget initiative referred to above. At present, the company itself can simply appoint the trustees to what is supposed to be an employee shareholder trust. Further, the trustees can be removed at any time. This at a time when all corporate governance commissions have agreed that shareholders should be encouraged to vote at AGMs, including on Directors' pay and remuneration packages. Yet company directors can remove the trustees who vote these shares—it is supposed to be the other way round!

Democratising these employee shareholder trusts would not only help solve the long running problem of corporate governance in Britain—that the majority of shareholders take no interest in the companies they own[6]—it would also help the Chancellor achieve what he hoped to from his initiative. Employee shareholder trusts will engender a greater sense of commitment to the firm from the trust members if the trust has a genuine voice in how the company is run. Proposals to do just this are currently being worked up by a commission with representatives from the CBI, TUC and the Industrial Society[7]. The

Government needs to engage actively in this work.

There is currently strong public support for the eminently sensible measure of renationalising Railtrack. If Government is not prepared to take this step, it should at least demand equity in return for any further subsidies. It is somewhat out of character for a government that is cautious on public spending to be giving away taxpayers money with nothing in return. More positive are reports that the Government is to insist upon the appointment of a public interest director on the Board of Railtrack. This is to be welcomed and should be generalised to all firms in which there is a genuine public interest, with directors coming from national, regional or local government as appropriate.

There are then a number of areas where rapid and significant progress could be made in the second term. Measures to boost productivity, such as encouraging firms to invest in their work-force through the creation of 'high commitment work systems', should be a priority. There needs to be more practical support for innovation, particularly in order to enhance the capacity of under-performing regions. The corporate governance of UK firms must be improved, not least by giving statutory backing to the existing code of practice, by supporting the current initiative to create democratic employee shareholder trusts as active corporate citizens, and by facilitating the election or appointment of public interest directors. Finally, a radical second term Government must ensure that taxation policy reduces rather than exacerbates income inequality.

These steps would be popular and would improve the functioning of the economy. Several could be taken relatively quickly and cheaply. All this good work would be put at risk, though, if the economy were pushed into recession by high interest rate and high exchange rate policies whether resulting from the Bank of England or the European Central Bank. Politics must remain in command.

References

1   Public spending as a proportion of national income at the end of the fourth year of the Labour Government was the lowest for 27 years, at 38.7 per cent compared to John Major's 41.4 per cent and Margaret Thatcher's 43.0 per cent.

2   See J Michie and M Sheehan Quinn, *Labour Market Flexibility, Human Resource Management and Corporate Performance*, Birkbeck Working Paper 00/02 (forthcoming in the *British Journal of Management*, 2001)

3   See C Oughton, M Landabaso and K Morgan, *The Regional Innovation Paradox: Innovation Policy and Industrial Policy*, Birkbeck Working Paper 00/04 (forthcoming in the *Journal of Technology Transfer*, 2002)

4   Military R&D does OK; overall, the UK spends 2.4 per cent of its GDP on defence as against the European NATO average of 2.1 per cent.

5   60 per cent of Britain's biggest companies are not complying with the Code's requirements for controlling Directors' pay and bonuses (CIS survey, May 2001).

6   In most countries, the majority of a company's shares will be voted at the AGM. In Britain the majority will not.

7   For details see J Michie and C Oughton, *Employees Direct: Shareholder Trusts, Business Performance and Corporate Governance*, Mutuo 2001.

5| **Work** Richard Reeves

Work blips faintly on today's political radar. None of the political parties have made more than a half-hearted bid to be the party of work and even Labour, the party of labour, has put education, public services, the eradication of child poverty and macro-economic stability at the top of its agenda.

It used to be so different. Remember the power of the 'Labour isn't working' poster and the fear that gripped the Conservative party when the jobless total breached one million in Thatcher's first term. Now, with most people who want to work in work, a minimum wage and social charter in place to protect them, better rights for parents who want time with their children and a New Deal providing at least some sort of bridge out of unemployment, work just is not politically exciting any more. The action is elsewhere.

In part this is because the worst fears of the 1990s—in particular that the future would be one of 'jobless growth'—have not been fulfilled. Jeremy Rifkin's influential The End of Work, published in 1995, turned out to be one of the most inaccurate of all the 'End Of' books. Information technology has not, as he forecast, thrown millions onto the scrapheap. (Neither has it created many jobs—but that is another story.)

Late capitalism can be accused of many crimes, but an inability to generate demand for goods and services which in turn require employment is not one of them. Labour markets without absurd amounts of regulation in economies demonstrating reasonable growth create jobs. It is that boring. Of course no-one should rule out a downswing which revives the spectre of mass joblessness—as Storm Peterson says, 'it is difficult to predict, especially the future'—but it seems unlikely in the short to medium term.

All of which explains why employment has remained in the 'Important but Dull' section of the political filing cabinet: the Financial Times' analysis of the party manifestos for the 2001 election had no section for employment. The bizarre lumping of the cuckoo employment into the Department for Education nest has hardly helped either. But work remains as central as ever to people's quality of life. We spend more of our waking hours working than engaged in any other activity. After eating and sex, work is the most commonly shared experience of adult life. The nature of our work has a profound impact on self-esteem, mental health, family life and financial security.

If the challenge for Labour's first term was to tackle unemployment, the challenge for the second is to wage war on bad employment. This will require a significant shift in mindset. Labour politicians remain, by and large, stuck in a quantitative view of work: that success is measured in terms of numbers in jobs, pay and pensions. These remain critical but they are not where the progressive challenges now lie. They are necessary components of a centre-left manifesto for work, but not sufficient.

It is the qualitative agenda that is now the most pressing. This is not to say that there is not more to do to protect and enhance the rights of workers. But the key battles are around workplace cultures, rather than workplace pay schemes, gender rather than weekly hours, progression prospects rather than redundancy laws.

Before the 1997 election Gordon Brown said he was striving for 'full and fulfilling employment'. At the time cynics thought he simply wanted to avoid straightforwardly pledging full employment—that he was hedging the promise. But Brown's aspiration was precisely the right one. With the first part of his ambition in sight, it is time to focus on the second.

Issues which are traditionally seen as 'soft' with regard to work—communication, meaning, progression, freedom from harassment, diversity—are actually the hard reality of modern work. 'A friendly working environment' consistently tops polls asking people what they most want from work. The most commonly cited reason for leaving a job is dislike of a line manager. Four out of five workers do not want the rigidity of the nine to five. These can be dismissed as trivial issues compared to the heroic battles to be fought over pay, working time, pension rights, union recognition and so on. They may require more imaginative political responses than legislation. But they are just as important.

The four key challenges now facing Labour in terms of work are:

- improving the quality of working experience
- enhancing prospects for upwards mobility
- increasing workers' autonomy
- promoting genuine gender equality

A renewed emphasis on the quality of work for workers is not as far removed from Labour's history as you might think. Karl Marx (whose economic analyses of labour relations under capitalism is enjoying a new vogue now that the political sting has been taken out) was also an acute observer of the sociology of work. A key concept of Marxist thought is the 'alienation' of the worker from his or her work. Here is how Marx defines it:

'What, then, constitutes the alienation of labour? First, the fact that labour is external to the worker, i.e. it does not belong to his essential being; that in his work he does not affirm himself but denies himself; does not feel content but unhappy; does not develop his physical and mental energy but mortifies his body and ruins his mind.'

One of the most brutal inequalities in the labour market is still between those who are 'alienated' from their labour, those for whom the work is not part of their 'essential being', and those who are in truly rewarding jobs. So part of the challenge for Labour is to reduce the level of alienation at work, to remove the barriers to a relationship with work that goes beyond the payslip. It is not just about getting people into work; it is about ensuring they get more out of it, too.

The key elements of a high-quality working life are: freedom from harassment and discrimination; a sociable and interactive environment; consultation and information about change; a chance to rise up the occupational ladder; and control over working time.

At first sight many of the qualitative work issues look beyond the reach of government. How do you legislate for more friend-liness? And it is certainly true that it is company cultures, at least as much as legislative frameworks, that need to be altered.

However, Labour can use laws to send signals and can enforce existing ones more rigorously. For example, the laws protecting people from discrimination are used erratically, and there are none covering sexuality and age (there is a European directive on the way). Discrimination poisons working environments as well as stunting career progression. Immediate protection on age and sexuality and a high-profile, vigorous campaign against discrim-ination should be a second-term priority. Similar campaigns should be waged against bullying and harassment in the work-place. It would help if the political workplace—parliament—were put in order, too. The outdated hours and voting systems and a continuing 'boys club' culture send a deeply regressive message about the kinds of work environments our political leaders support. Tess Kingham, who stood down in the 2001 election, described the House of Commons as 'bullying' and 'claustrophic'.

Labour can also promote greater awareness of the rights that already exist in the workplace and patrol them more effectively. John Knell, my colleague at The Industrial Society, has called for the establishment of a Quality of Working Life Agency, which would be a partnership between ACAS, the National Association of Citizens Advice Bureaux and the National Audit Office. The Agency would gather information on workplace practices and act as a Government-backed advocate of better quality workplaces.

Another area where Labour can pull a change lever at work is employee consultation. Clearly defined obligations on management to consult their workforce on major changes makes for better decision-making and a modest re-balancing of power. But it also makes workers feel better about their work: survey after survey shows that feeling involved and informed makes workers much more positive about their jobs. This may be the best reason of all for strengthening consultation rights.

The ultimate aim is to improve workplace cultures. Legislation is but one weapon, and frequently an ineffective one. In this area, as in many others, the most powerful mechanisms for change are a mixture of example-setting, advertising campaigns, partnership, persuasion and naming-and-shaming. It is a messier kind of politics than the traditional approach of legislating to solve a defined problem: but Labour now has to get under the skin of the British workplace and that requires a more diverse armoury.

Labour is the party of progress and should be the party of work. The prospects of progress at work should therefore be a central concern. Modern work has to be meritocratic—not just for social reasons, but because the rigours of greater market competition allow no room for incompetence at the top or wasted talent at the bottom.

The signs are that there is a great deal to be done on the mobility front. Over the last few decades, the chances of upward mobility during the course of a working life have actually declined. Thirty-nine per cent of workers in the bottom quarter of the earnings distribution in 1977 had vaulted into the top half by 1983, but just 26 per cent made the upwards journey between 1991 and 1997. Data will soon be available on whether there was more movement during Labour's first term.

Entry to higher-status occupations now occurs much earlier in life, often straight from university or graduate school. Educational qualifications have become the gateway to prosperity and progress at work. The good jobs are sewn up almost from the start of the race. But not everyone can make it to university—even if they are bright enough, social background, a clash of learning styles or short-term financial pressure can rule out a college education. There are, then, three key policy concerns for the Government: lifelong learning; a new New Deal; and democratising networks.

The acquisition of qualifications in later life is clearly key to the prospects of upwards movement, especially with the new emphasis on the letters after an applicant's name. Labour's Individual Learning Accounts (ILAs), which were toyed with in the first term, have to be more energetically pursued. There are plenty of able people who do not thrive in the academic system and so find their path blocked in later life. ILAs can provide second chances for these people.

At the same time, the New Deal, which has been modestly successful in helping young people into work but much less successful in keeping them there, has to be reconfigured. The erosion of career ladders and diminishing chances of upwards mobility mean that New Dealers are in danger of swapping unemployment for low-paid work for life.

Moving people from welfare to work is not enough for the second term. A hands-on approach to career development and market navigation is also required. Max Nathan argues that the key to reshaping employment strategies is attachment[1]: helping jobs and money stick to places and connecting people to working lives. The New Deal has to be recast as an Attachment Agency for both employers and jobseekers, developing long term links with both groups. The Agency would provide proactive human resource services for companies, moving people into work, and establish career development and support over the working life, both inside and outside the firm.

Thirdly, the Government has to look at ways of opening up the networks that determine—perhaps increasingly determine—career prospects. It is well established that most recruitment is done on the grapevine. This is true at the bottom of the labour market, where half of the people who move from unemployment to work hear about the job by word of mouth, and the top, where chairmen and CEOs are recommended by trusted intermediaries.

It seems likely that the power of the personal network will increase. The skills that are required in many jobs—social skills, creative thinking, partnership management—are harder to detect through formal recruitment procedures. Hiring someone you know and trust—or who someone you know and trust knows and trusts—is an effective strategy.

These grapevines have been with us forever, and will be around forever. The key is to find ways of democratising them, of opening networks up to the widest possible audience. Employers have an enormous responsibility here: to think beyond their usual, safe networks and reach out to a wider recruitment pool. There is some help the Government can offer too. Mentoring— where someone in a good job helps an unemployed person or disadvantaged youngster—is seen as providing support, advice and a new horizon. It also gives the 'mentee' something even more important: access to a high-quality network. Their mentor can recommend them to people they would have no reason to meet otherwise. Labour should set out to create a labour market of a million mentors, perhaps with some tax incentives for firms to release staff time.

Employees also want more control over their work—and especially over where and when they work. In a recent survey of almost 1,500 UK workers, nearly a third believed that the freedom to work any time of day or night would define their ideal job. A further 50 per cent wanted the ability to work flexible hours between 07.30am and 7.30pm.

Labour should not be waging war on long hours. It should be waging war on fixed hours. By and large it is no longer the poorest who are chained to their machines or desks. In the 1890s, the poorest ten per cent of men were working two hours a day more than the richest; by the 1990s, the richest ten per cent were working longer hours than the poorest. The politics of working time has changed dramatically—it is middle class dual earner households who are putting in the (largely unpaid) hours now. Employment remains stuck in a mindset that sees hours spent in place X between hours Y and Z as the measure of work. Cultures of 'presenteeism' poison workplaces and, by extension, homes too.

The nature of much modern work does not fit with the nine to five. Thinking time, for example, is impossible to corral into set hours. Joanne Ciulla, a US academic, rightly says that applying yesterday's timekeeping to today's work creates discomfort: 'Perhaps what is most unsatisfying about modern work is that people frequently are paid not for what they produce, but for their time ... when maybe task orientation is more natural than time orientation.'

The Industrial Society called in its 2001 manifesto for a full-scale audit of the flexible benefits available to employees and for Treasury consideration of tax advantages for firms which trust their staff to get their job done without outdated working time rigidities. Of course, central Government cannot pass laws to force firms to be flexible. But offering incentives to those with a 21st century view of working time sends a clear message to British employers. Giving people a right to switch to a part-time job after parental leave would also promote a more fluid approach to working time. For it is control over time—time sovereignty—that today's workers want and need.

Perhaps the greatest test for Labour's second-term radicalism, at least in relation to work, will be its drive for gender equality. The most profound and progressive change in the workplace in recent decades has been the increase in number of women, who will shortly be in the majority. And while some professional separation remains, women are entering the upper echelons of management and the professions previously virtually reserved for men: there are now more women than men studying law and medicine.

The rising number of women holds out the hope of a better working environment for us. They are demanding more flexible working patterns, which better fit post-industrial economics, more interpersonal styles of work, and more meaning from their work. As writer Elizabeth Perle McKenna says, women 'are the most transformative and revolutionary group because we have to redefine work.'

But the redefinition just is not happening. The pay gap remains stubbornly stuck at around 20 per cent. Women are forced into male working cultures—and expected to embrace them with enthusiasm if they want to succeed. Often they must give up on the idea of family too: most male senior managers have children; most female ones do not. Rather than work being feminised, women who want to get ahead are being masculinised.

There is a now a very real danger that after decades of progress the number of women in the labour market will begin to drop, as talented female workers turn away in justifiable disgust from outdated cultures, structures and work patterns. As sociologist Heather Hopfl says, 'the period in which women sought to define themselves as quasi-men is coming to an end'.

There is much that the Government can do to support working women, in addition to the considerable steps taken since 1997. Statutory gender pay audits, while changing nothing tangible in themselves, may begin to change attitudes within firms. A right to return part-time to work after maternity leave and better-paid maternity leave will also help.

But if Labour is serious about gender equality, nothing short of a revolution in attitudes and policy is required—one which sees men as just as important to the gender issue as women (so, yes, renaming and retasking the Women's Unit is a good idea.) Right now, women are being asked to act as the primary parent of the family but also as an equal contributor to the paid labour market: to bring home the bacon and cook it. As long as women are taking more time out than men and are more constrained by childcare responsibilities than men, they will lose out to men at work.

Only the introduction of paternity leave at a level equivalent to that available for maternity will level the playing field at work, as well as home. It is time for a fundamental redistribution of unpaid work between men and women—which means legal rights to time off for fathers as well as mothers. For starters that means six weeks at 90 per cent pay, which makes the current plan for two weeks at perhaps £100 a week seem like the tinkering around the edges.

Equalising paternity and maternity leave might seem a utopian idea: but for a cost of about £1 billion—a fraction of the cost of the New Deal—a social revolution would have been bought. For only when the phrases 'career man' or 'working father' have ceased to sound silly will women have a shot at equal status in the office and boardroom. Women have to be truly equal partners in the workplace (which means men being equal partners at home), helping to reinvent and redesign work that is better, fairer and more autonomous for all of us. Without a serious drive for gender equality, the prospects of an exciting second term on work-related issues are negligible.

The buoyancy of the UK labour market combined with the careful underpinning of employee rights achieved in Labour's first term make for extraordinary opportunities in the second term. Issues which in other economic and political circumstances would seem peripheral but which go to the core of our working lives—flexibility, consultation, progression, respect, equality—can be addressed at last.

References

1   See *Getting Attached—A New New Deal for the Unemployed*, Fabian Society, forthcoming.

6| **Quality of Life** Ian Christie & Ken Warpole

Labour Governments have had the misfortune to experience two winters of discontent. The first, in 1978-79, proved lethal at the polls; the second, in 2000-01, did not. Paralysis on the railways, fuel protests, funeral pyres for livestock, disastrous flooding and growing frustration among users and providers of public services—all created a national bout of Seasonal Affective Disorder. But the weakness of the Opposition and the lack of an obvious connection between the problems combined to let Labour off the hook.

And of course, the state of the economy has been decisive. Against lazy talk about our 'third world' public services, it has to be said that Millennial Britain has in many ways never had it so good. Unemployment and inflation are relatively low and, for the affluent, private quality of life is high. For most people, the winter of discontent was largely an inconvenience or a spectacle rather than a personal crisis. So, 'it's the economy, stupid'?

Only up to a point. Private consumption and choice go a long way to satisfying us that we have a good quality of life, but there are limits. Quality of life depends also on the quality of public infrastructures, the environment, and good governance: things we cannot buy for ourselves. The experiences of the Millennial winter reminded us that private affluence is no shield against the degradation of the public realm and natural environment.

The floods might be a preview of climate disruption, driven in part by the consumption choices of individuals and capable of being handled only by collective effort. The collapse of Railtrack showed that a neglected railway has consequences for the car-driving electorate too. The foot and mouth outbreak is another signal that intensive farming is straining our relationship with the land to breaking point. And all of these issues highlighted the inability of politicians to speak honestly about the connections between consumption, public goods and the price we should pay in tax for decent services.

The experiences of 2000-01 point to the growing importance of quality of life as a central theme of modern politics. This holds lessons for Labour about the present culture of policy-making and debate:

- The quality of the public realm and public services have been allowed to deteriorate not only during Tory rule but also in Labour's first term, despite all the good that the Government has done and its good intentions for a revitalisation of public services. Yet the connection between the need for better public goods and for an adult approach to taxation has not been made.

- Privatisation and individualisation of our ideas about 'quality of life' have developed to such an extent that it is now extremely difficult for politicians to articulate a vision of the common good and the dependence of individual well-being on the social and environmental commons. Yet the most troubling political issues confronting us demand precisely that we do make these connections.

- Many modern environmental problems point to major threats to the quality of life of our children, grandchildren and generations beyond. If we wish to avert or mitigate these risks, action must be taken now. But our current political culture seems incapable of responding.

The Millennial winter delivered shocks to ideas and policies entrenched over the last 20 years in government. For example, the idea that economic growth is essentially the same as progress in quality of life, or that we can have cheap food and cheap transport without wider collective consequences. Or that we can have a low tax economy with high quality public goods, and that public services can be relentlessly reformed, criticised and squeezed in the name of efficiency without compensating investment and morale-building.

The system is being shaken for good reason: it is based on a fatal under-estimation of the importance of the public realm and collective well-being to individual welfare. Making progress and securing a better quality of life for all depends on discarding many of the dogmas and blind spots inherited from Thatcherism. Can Labour grasp the challenges of the politics of quality of life— the ultimate 'joined up' issue?

For all the gains that have been made, Labour's approach does not offer a coherent vision of what needs to be done to restore the public realm and connect private well-being to the quality of the commons. We suggest areas for action and reflection in the second term—and well beyond—that could mean genuine, sustainable gains in quality of life.

Labour has acted to improve the economic welfare of the poorest—the essential precondition for a better individual quality of life. They have also focused on the collective conditions that keep people poor and 'excluded', and which fiscal measures targeted at individuals and their families cannot tackle. There is a solid basis for the programme of neighbourhood renewal and the plans for an urban renaissance to attract people to live and work in cities, to the benefit of the environment, community life and economic activity.

Whether these plans succeed depends to a large extent on the wider context of governance of public services. But the approach is promising. It recognises the importance of caring for the local environment and removing the eyesores and other signs of neglect that depress spirits and economic prospects. It focuses on creating reassuring neighbourhoods in which streets are reclaimed from traffic jams, from crime and from filth. It makes the connections between local morale, social relationships, public spaces and economic 'inclusion'. All this suggests a policy that could harness the 'social promise of environmentalism' by making the links between revitalised places and better lives[1].

The new indicators of quality of life represent a significant first attempt at joining up disparate areas of policy, recognising that growth and consumption are not the same as gains in well-being, and that they can have counter-productive impacts—from congestion to climate disruption. Tony Blair's introduction to Labour's Quality of Life strategy states the rarely-acknowledged obvious, and is practically revolutionary in consequence:

> The last hundred years have seen a massive increase in the wealth of this country and the well being of its people. But focusing solely on economic growth risks ignoring the impact—both good and bad—on people and on the environment…. Now … there is a growing realisation that real progress cannot be measured by money alone…. But in the past, governments have seemed to forget this. Success has been measured by economic growth—GDP—alone. We have failed to see how our economy, our environment and our society are all one. And that delivering the best possible quality of life for us all means more than concentrating solely on economic growth.[2]

For decades, politicians have been fixated on the idea that their main goal is to run the economy so that citizens—seen primarily as consumers—can increase spending power and 'choice':

> Today raising the level of consumer spending is gener-

ally regarded as the key political objective for any
government: the principal measure of its success and—
according to the conventional wisdom of psephological
prediction—the best indicator of its likely vote.[3]

Labour is caught between recognition of the importance of quality of life and the conventional wisdom. The tax question illustrates this. Higher tax revenues are needed to restore the public realm, but that clashes with the instinct to pledge to the voter-consumer more cash for consumption. Hence the dispiriting 2001 general election debates, in which no higher ambition could be announced than the desire to cut taxes or at least not increase the 'tax burden'. The insight expressed in the Quality of Life strategy and which is embedded in Labour's best ideas for public renewal is not yet the organising principle of its politics. Instead it is a proposition undermined by concessions to 'business as usual'.

The second term needs to see a connection between policies for well-being and the problems signalled by the long winter of discontent. The unease they generated stems from fear that the skies have been darkening with chickens coming home to roost. Many of them were hatched decades ago, and they have bred so well because of the very success of the consumer economy.

- Affluent societies breed individualism, which constrains politicians' courage in calling for tax contributions from the affluent—who are electorally decisive—and from the big corporate sector, which is perceived to be 'mobile' and capable of withdrawing investment[4].
- Societies such as the UK and USA have given priority to private affluence and have weakened the financial and human basis of the public realm. This breeds mistrust in public services and a tendency to exit from them if possible, and makes it harder still to build up support for Continental levels of tax to pay for Continental standards of public

service.

- All industrial societies produce environmental impacts through technical advances and unprecedented consumption. No-one is responsible because we all are—'the buck stops everywhere'. Tackling diffuse pollution means challenging key elements of mass consumerism such as car dependence and cheap food, and so politicians shy away[5].

- Affluent societies produce similar perverse effects in the social realm[6]. For example, 'hypermobility' worsens pollution and congestion and puts strains on family life[7].

All these effects produce a widening gap between the conventional indicators of economic growth and the felt realities of quality of life. But politicians can only narrow the gap by appealing to a sense of common cause, trading immediate individual consumption against the common good. This can only be done by arguing that collective action—such as taxation—makes us all better off. This is politically risky, and it depends on public trust in government to collect and spend tax well. Such trust is in short supply: the restoration of trust in governance and trust in tax is a combined challenge[8].

Labour's positive record on quality of life has been undermined by its failure to make these connections. Here are some of the main areas where fresh thinking is needed.

- **Maintenance matters**

  By the time Government woke up to the wretched state of repair of the railways and hospital wards, it was too late to score any 'quick wins' to give confidence that services would be renewed urgently. Labour needs to confront a deep problem in British administration—contempt for maintenance of infrastructure, and obsession with capital spending at the expense of revenue funding. The state of the London Tube tells us that, for decades, the Treasury has thought it a good deal to save on maintenance of an essential system. Our rundown parks reveal how their upkeep has been removed from council budgets, with the consequence that once-reassuring spaces have become neglected and threatening. Across the public services, the staff, skills and money for the basic work of mending, keeping watch and preventing decay, have been begrudged. If Labour's spending strategy fails to tackle this blind spot then problems will return with a vengeance.

■ **Joined up policies do not join up enough**

Joining up of ideas on quality of life has far to go. Environmental issues play only a minor role in social exclusion programmes. We have had an urban white paper and a rural one, but few links between them. Foot and mouth was tackled as if farming were separate from the rest of the economy, with wretched effects on quality of life as well as incomes. Labour's emphasis on family values and the work-life balance sits uneasily with its obsession with labour productivity. And the Quality of Life indicators are not obviously linked to the core business of government—the Budget process, the ten-year spending plans, and the allocation of funds to local government.

■ **'Community' is for everyone**

One unwanted side-effect of the Neighbourhood Renewal Strategy and the analysis of social exclusion has been the way in which 'community' now refers to places where social capital has been eroded, and 'neighbourhood' has become shorthand for a place that needs to be regenerated. The message that begins to emerge from this discourse is that 'community' and 'neighbourhood' are only for the poor. But both require the active work of the affluent, recognising that the haves and have-nots have some common cause.

■ **New Labour and fun**

New Labour has been a fun-free zone, good at reporting on performance indicators but bad at conveying any sense of brio that is not sponsored by business. Ever since the Dome flopped, there has been a grim focus on Prudence, Productivity and Performance. The foot and mouth episode spoke volumes about the joylessness of our public realm: almost the only action that seemed to go without a hitch was the zealous closure of footpaths. And ministers appealed to people to head for the countryside on the basis that attractions were 'open for business'. The thought that people might be avoiding the countryside because it was closed to spiritual and physical refreshment in woods and on fells, rather than because of lack of opportunities for spending, did not occur. Labour conveys a dour vision of the Good Society it has in mind.

These issues need to be addressed in a number of ways. First, we need more effective joined up thinking and policymaking, and a renewal of confidence in the public sector, as preconditions for improving the quality of the commons. Measures could include a Task Force on Better Regulation for the public sector, designed to reduce the burden of paperwork and move from complex accountability to the centre to what Ed Mayo of the New Economics Foundation has called greater local horizontal accountability for service delivery.

Further, an early task for the new Sustainable Development Commission should be an audit of perverse incentives and subsidies across government, identifying measures that damage the environment and quality of life. This should include an investigation of the bias against maintenance in public finance, and recommendations for improving staffing and conditions of public services to ensure that failures of maintenance are not repeated.

Ministers should use—and be seen to use—public services more. In particular, an insistence that their cars be replaced for one month a year by public transport would be salutary and popular with the public.

In its second term, Labour should vigorously pursue its urban renaissance programme, as well as its policies for the renewal of market towns and of neighbourhoods. These programmes should be linked to measures to increase local control over funding, choice of priorities and evaluation. The new Local Strategic Partnerships for regeneration and local well-being are vital here. LSPs should be the focus, say once a year, for a participatory 'second chamber', a festival of debate we could call a House of the Local Commons.

Local authority and public sector careers should offer more incentives to senior and up-and-coming people to commit themselves to a place, learning to see its problems and potential in a rounded way, rather than always seeing advancement in moving on. Too often 'the community' in deprived areas must deal with an ever-changing cast of public officials as well as of initiatives and funding schemes.

Lottery funding, council budgets and regeneration money should be committed to ensure a massive expansion in parks, community woodlands, public gardens, public art and playgrounds, and in the staff needed to maintain them. We need many small-scale projects done well over time, enhancing thousands of neighbourhoods.

We also need New Towns to house the millions of new householders expected over the next two decades. The garden cities and new towns of mid 20th century unleashed much good design and building, as well as storing up many problems. Hard lessons have been learned from this experience and, since we cannot avoid building new settlements, we should aim to do it as well as we can. A new generation of new towns, built to provide reassuring and enjoyable environments with sustainable use of energy and with a focus on minimising waste, is possible. Developments such as the new mixed housing estate 'BedZed' in Sutton show the way. Just as the prewar and postwar developments at their best created a 'social democratic sublime', so such innovations point to a 21st century 'sustainable sublime' in the built environment[9]. Labour should have the courage to back such a vision.

Labour should do more to 'reclaim the streets'. Much of the 10 Year Plan for Transport emphasises big investment in long-haul rail, air, and road capacity. Walking, cycling, sharing cars, and schemes to reduce the need for 'hypermobility', play a marginal role. But many such developments can be afforded for the price of the big schemes, which will simply add to pollution, and will bring only temporary relief from congestion. We should focus on gradual measures to reduce car dependence and long-haul travel, and to make streets liveable for walking, cycling and children's play.

But Labour also needs to 'reclaim the fields'. Foot and mouth and BSE call for a basic rethink of farming. Redirecting subsidy to organic conversion, and scrapping subsidies for intensive farming, should be priorities. We can reclaim many fields for wildlife, woodlands, sustainable crops, orchards, recreation and dwellings, to the benefit of quality of life.

All these ideas could help create more resilient and sustainable systems of governance and consumption to underpin our future well-being. Without such measures and a truly joined-up vision of quality of life, Labour's planned restoration of the public realm risks being undermined by more shocks to our life support systems of the kind we experienced in 2000-01. In term two, the lessons of the Millennial winter of discontent need to be heeded, and the work of joining up individual and collective quality of life must be tackled in earnest. Only connect—or things fall apart.

References

1   Ken Worpole, *In our Backyard: the social promise of environmentalism*, Green Alliance 2000.
2   Tony Blair, foreword to *A better quality of life*, DETR 1999.
3   Michael Jacobs, 'Quality of Life', M Jacobs (ed), *Greening the Millennium*, Blackwell 1997; on quality of life and sustainable development see also Ian Christie and Michael Jacobs, 'The Personal is Political (again)', A Coote (ed), *The New Gender Agenda*, IPPR 2000; Michael Jacobs, *The Green Economy*, Pluto Press 1991; Diane Warburton (ed), *Community and Sustainable Development*, Earthscan 1998; Ian Christie and Diane Warburton, *From Here to Sustainability*, Earthscan/Real World 2001.
4   JK Galbraith, *The Culture of Contentment*, Penguin 1992; Colin Crouch, *Coping with Post-democracy*, Fabian Society 2000.
5   Tom Burke, 'The buck stops everywhere', *New Statesman* 20 June 1997.
6   Fred Hirsch, *Social Limits to Growth*, Routledge 1977.
7   John Adams, *Hypermobility*, OECD 2000.
8   Michael Jacobs, *Paying for Progress: a new politics of tax for public spending*, Fabian Society 2000.
9   Ken Worpole, *Here Comes the Sun*, Reaktion Books 2000; Ken Worpole and Liz Greenhalgh, *The Richness of Cities*, Comedia/Demos 2000; Roger Levett and Ian Christie, *Towards the Ecopolis*, Comedia/Demos 1999.

7| **Narrative** Michael Jacobs

This may come as a surprise to observers of politics, but one of the characteristics of Labour's first term was a fierce ideological battle. This was not, of course, a battle between ideologies. The Labour Party's icy self-discipline over recent years—surely one of the more remarkable political facts of this period—ensured that barely a ripple of dissent, let alone the splash of philosophical argument, disturbed the unnatural calm of the Government's waters. No: the ideological conflict that raged was over whether or not to have an ideology at all.

One might characterise this battle as the Third Way vs the Big Tent. On the one hand, Tony Blair seemed desperate to claim that New Labour's programme was not just intellectually coherent but represented a distinctive philosophy in its own right. Yet at the same time New Labour went out of its way to ensure the widest possible support for its government by rejecting traditional philosophical distinctions. There was to be no truck with ideological 'dogma'—'what matters is what works', ministers insisted.

There are good reasons why New Labour should have this ambivalent stance towards philosophical clarity. Axiomatically, defining one's position defines some people in and others out. Making clear what you stand for simultaneously reveals what you don't—and therefore makes enemies as well as supporters.

By contrast, the inclusiveness offered by philosophical ambiguity maximises political support—with potentially handsome electoral payoff, as Labour's landslide appears to prove.

Yet this comes at a price. For breadth and depth are here in conflict. Lack of ideological definition brings many on board, but few with conviction. Natural Labour supporters are uninspired; there is acquiescence but little enthusiasm. Wider public support for the Government is found to have shallow roots which might easily be swept away if circumstances change. The landslide covers a large area, but closer inspection may reveal that only a thin layer of topsoil has moved.

Does any of this matter in the second term? Are not the broad coalition and the landslide majority enough? The answers are almost certainly that it does, and that they are not. The second Labour administration will need to define its ideological position much more clearly and boldly—even if this means sacrificing some of the breadth of its political support.

There are two basic arguments in favour of greater ideological clarity. The first is that, whilst it is easy to win elections against a feeble Opposition when the economy is doing well, Labour will face much tougher challenges in the second term. Economic conditions may well become much less benign. A downturn imported from across the Atlantic may not be certain but can certainly not be ruled out. If rising incomes begin to stall and unemployment starts to increase once again, the Government's reputation for economic competence, its strongest card, may come to look more shaky. At the same time the excuses for failure to deliver better public services will have run out. The blame can no longer be cast onto the last administration when the last administration was itself. With investment in public services the key message of the election, public expectations of the second term will almost certainly run ahead of what can realistically be achieved: the risk is of compounded disillusion. And all this will be conducted in the face of a media which will almost certainly become more hostile with every passing month, taking upon itself the role of unofficial Opposition in the absence of an effective official one.

In these circumstances a strong ideological 'narrative' will be a vital bolster to the Government's political position. A strong narrative will help to explain what it is trying to do and where it is going, even when its success in getting there is not as apparent as it would like. When hospitals and schools are not improving as fast (or as noticeably) as the public want, when the railways are still mired in under-invested disorganisation, when the trend of unemployment is up not down, a clearly articulated philosophy will help to explain, nevertheless, what Labour believes in and where it is headed. When times are hard it can act as a kind of shock absorber for public discontent, giving people confidence in the Government's direction even as the bumps on the road getting there are felt. In short, it can make public support less dependent on the facts of change themselves and more on the values and intention behind them.

This was, after all, Margaret Thatcher's great triumph. Even when her policies stuttered, her public standing for most of the 1980s remained, for it was based as much on what she stood for as on what she actually achieved. For Labour now, philosophical clarity will inevitably lose it some support; some people will fall off the coalition bandwagon. But those that remain will be stronger and more steadfast in their commitment.

In turn this leads to the third argument for ideological clarity. Articulating a clear philosophy is necessary to win the hearts and minds as well as the votes of the public. Labour should not simply wish to transform the country, but to change the people as well. Just as Thatcher sought to remake the British public in her own image—individualistic, materialistic, anti-European—so Labour should be seeking to bring out all the solid social democratic values which equally (and now much more strongly) beat in the British public's heart—belief in tax-funded public services, in equality of opportunity, in a progressive and liberal outlook. For this is the real goal which Labour can now seek to achieve: to shift the entire political culture and mindset of the UK towards the left.

The election shows that it has already begun to do this. But if this shift is to be permanent, the Government must talk as well as act. Labour must not simply spend more on public services but must explain the values that underpin universal, tax-funded provision. It must not only redistribute income but promote the idea of a more equal society. It must not only be more liberal in areas such as criminal justice, asylum and freedom of information but show why this makes us a better, more civilised community. If it can locate its reforms in a clearly articulated political philosophy, Labour has the opportunity to create a new public consensus in Britain—fit for the modern age, and firmly planted on the left of centre.

The question is, can New Labour find a coherent ideological narrative of this kind?

It is now fairly obvious what such a narrative will not be. The Third Way may, as Tony Giddens has argued, be a helpful label for similar kinds of policy approaches practised by centre-left governments all over the world[1]; but it is not a political philosophy. There are a number of reasons why the Third Way does not perform the required philosophical task. But one deserves our attention here: it concerns the relationships between means and ends.

One of Tony Blair's most insistent arguments has been that in terms of philosophy only political ends—goals and values—matter; there should be no 'dogmas' concerning the means or policy approaches one uses to realise them. This is what marks the Third Way out from old ideas about social democracy. 'The fundamentalist left made nationalisation and state control an end in itself, hardening policy prescription into ideology,' the Prime Minister writes in his Fabian pamphlet.

> [But] what matters is what works to give effect to our values. Some commentators are disconcerted by this insistence on fixed values and goals but pragmatism about means. There are even claims that it is unprincipled. But I believe that a crucial dimension of the Third Way is that policies flow from values, not vice versa.[2]

The last point is clearly right. But there is a more fundamental error in the argument. This is the presumption that means—policy approaches—have no philosophical content in themselves; they are simply neutral agents of value-based ends. But means embody values too. It matters whether governments promote markets or regulation to achieve their ends; whether they use public sector institutions or private firms, universal welfare benefits or means-tested ones, centralised or decentralised governance. It matters because different policies and institutions create different kinds of society. Even if, in terms of particular policy goals, different 'means' of getting there can be equally effective or efficient, the outcomes will differ, since the outcomes must include the nature of the social relations and values which different policy approaches embody.

It is simply not true, for example, that there is no philosophical difference between using public sector institutions and using private firms to deliver public services. This is not in terms of their efficiency—though there may be differences here too. It is in terms of their values, and the kind of society which they help to create. Public sector institutions embody an ideal of public service, defined by the need of the service user not his or her market power. They are owned by and give institutional form to the idea of community—they are 'ours'. (Think of the way we talk about 'our schools' and 'our hospitals', and the public's powerful sense of ownership of the NHS. We don't talk about our

Tesco or our Railtrack.) Public institutions create a 'public realm', a space in which the huge diversity of individuals who make up society come together to provide for their collective needs and in which non-market values rule. Having a strong public sector, and promoting its worth, is therefore an end in itself, not simply a means to other ends.

None of this is to preclude the use of the private sector in public service delivery, particularly where it can help to promote efficiency. It is simply to argue that a society in which public services were mainly provided by private firms—with merely a residual contract-defining public realm—would be very different from one in which the dominant institutions and values were public. It is not 'dogma' to be concerned about these kinds of outcomes: means are ends too.

We will return to this as a specific area of policy below. The point here is that political philosophies cannot simply be concerned with general ends or values; they have to be concerned with means as well. A clear ideological narrative must both define its goals properly—there are big differences between different interpretations of general objectives such as 'opportunity for all' and 'economic prosperity'—and it must define its dominant policy approaches too.

It is here in fact that a coherent ideological narrative for Labour's second term begins to form. It is one which sits well both with a 'New Labour' approach and connects to the longer tradition of social democracy.

The central tenet is very simple. It is a belief in government. Democratic government represents the community to which we belong, giving it institutional form. Government performs tasks and provides services which individuals on their own cannot. An active government is needed to shape and constrain the powerful forces of the global market and to protect us from its vagaries. Government is good.

In philosophical terms it is arguable that this is really what the 2001 election was about. Labour, believers in government, against a Conservative Party that fundamentally wishes to see (as its spokespeople helpfully let slip) a radically smaller state. It would be encouraging to interpret the result as a decisive vote in favour of active government.

Yet we cannot quite say that it was—not just because ideology was clearly not the principal motivating factor behind the Conservatives' defeat but because New Labour has not really made the full philosophical case for the active state. Yes, it does now make a strong argument for investment in public services. And in many ways the Government has adopted an 'active state' approach, full of initiatives and schemes of policy engineering. But at a rhetorical level, the basic worth and importance of government has not been New Labour's dominant idea.

To make it so, the first task is to set out what government is now for, its purpose and functions. There is a helpful Third Way trope that can be used here: the role of government today is neither that of the old left nor the new right. In the old days the left believed that governments could run the economy and manage people's lives. Governments owned the major industries, intervened strongly in economic demand and trade, provided people's homes and maintained large, uniform bureaucracies. We no longer believe that it can or should do these things. But on the other hand we do not accept either—as the new right argues—that it should have only a residual 'safety net and law and order' function.

Today, social democrats can say government has five core and vital roles. First, it provides the essential framework for a market economy. This is not laissez faire: it is the regulation of markets so as to promote competition and social and environmental protection. In today's global economy this must occur on an international scale as well as a national one: hence the importance of supranational government institutions such as the European Union and (with some reform) the World Trade Organisation. Consumer protection, labour standards and environmental regulation are all critical. At the same time an active government is needed to ensure that individuals can adapt to changing labour markets through education and training. It can help disadvantaged regions regenerate economic development. It can help support new technologies and industries. The economic role of the active state has changed but it has not diminished.

Second, government provides public services that the market cannot, or can only inequitably. Public services provide social goods which not only provide individuals with personal benefits but which shape the nature of society and bind us together within it.

Third, government is essential to mitigate market inequalities and provide genuine opportunity for self-development to all. Markets not only generate but perpetuate inequalities of income and wealth, which quickly solidify into social division. Only an active state can work against these: both by redistributing income through the taxation and benefit systems and by the active provision of 'opportunity-enhancing' services. As Labour has pioneered, many of these can now be provided directly as benefits from government to the individual: individual learning accounts, 'baby bonds' and matched savings schemes, support for childcare, maternity and paternity allowances, family support services and so on. By reducing inequalities government can help to generate a more socially cohesive society.

Fourth, government can protect the quality of life against the intrusions of the market economy. Increasingly, market competition is driving deeper into formerly non-market spheres. Working hours are getting longer and jobs more stressful, affecting family life and personal time. Environmental pollution and degradation are increasing. Local communities, particularly in urban areas, are being hollowed out. A crucial role for active government in the 21st century will be to mitigate these trends: regulating working time to help individuals find a better work-life balance; protecting and enhancing the natural environment; improving public spaces and the 'liveability' of urban environments; creating a sense of community belonging and civic pride.

Fifth, governments can help to create conditions of global security. Acting in concert, and through international institutions, governments can reduce conflict, protect the environment and help to eliminate poverty.

None of this is particularly new. But it provides a clear basis for an ideological narrative centred on the value and importance of government. Against the Conservative view that the role of the state should be reduced, Labour's social democratic narrative should show just how much we need government and how much it can do. Nearly all of Labour's current policies, and some new fields of activity such as quality of life and work-life balance, fit well within a narrative of this kind.

But at the same time a focus on the value of active government would require Labour to be bolder and clearer in some of the areas from which it flinched during the first term.

The first of these is taxation. Labour has been articulate in defence of public spending but it has been unwilling to make the other half of the case and argue positively for the value of taxation. This, now, must surely be done. For too long the British public have been encouraged to engage in a form of psychological denial: that at the same time they can have better public services and lower taxes[3]. Part of Labour's second term project must be finally to break free from this Thatcherite legacy. At 37 per cent, Britain takes 4 per cent less of its national income in tax than the EU average—the equivalent of £40bn a year. Making the case for government is in one sense to persuade the British to become a modern European country.

The ambiguities of Labour's first term need to be resolved in the field of business regulation. Labour's record is not as solely pro-business in this field as its critics often claim: the minimum wage, legislation on trade union rights and the climate change levy all represent significant incursions into business freedom. But at a rhetorical level the general attitude towards regulation was largely hostile.

Making the case for active government does not mean the imposition of a huge new interventionist agenda. But it does mean articulating the case for business to be regulated for the common good. Two key areas where this will become particularly important in the second term are the environment and working time, particularly flexible working and parental leave. Labour needs to show how the promotion of quality of life is as much the role of the state as narrower economic prosperity— even if sometimes this is opposed to the short-term interests of business.

The third area is the public sector. Labour has indicated that it will seek to increase the use of private firms in the delivery of public services. Undoubtedly, parts of the public sector perform badly and need to be improved. But this is true too of many private firms—Railtrack is hardly a shining example of private sector management; many other failing companies could also be cited. An ideological narrative of active government needs to uphold the worth of the public sector and the public realm even while setting about a vigorous programme of improving it.

Much will depend here on how and where the private sector is introduced. If private sector firms are used to benchmark good practice and provide a spur to improve the efficiency and dynamism of public sector management, this should be welcomed. But wholesale replacement of public by private providers would represent an attack on the public realm itself.

Use of private contractors to deliver easily-definable services such as refuse collection already occurs and is largely unobjectionable. But private firms making clinical judgements about health needs and educational priorities would introduce market values and motivations into the nature of public services themselves.

So an ideology of active government would represent a challenge as well as a support system for Labour in the second term. And a final point here can be made. Active government needs an active democracy. Government is not just administration: it is the exercise of power lent from the people and the resolution of political debate conducted among them. A strong public realm requires a democracy in which such debate can be exercised. So the completion of Labour's agenda of constitutional reform—in Parliament, through devolution and through local government renewal—is a crucial part of the narrative too.

It may seem odd to place such stress on how the Labour Government should talk rather than on how it should act. But talking—articulating ideals and values, persuading and educating—is a crucial and often neglected part of government. Only with a clear and defining ideological narrative will Labour achieve its historic mission to relocate the centre of gravity of British politics on the left. The transformation of Britain must occur not only in changes 'on the ground', but in the hearts and minds of the people.

References

1   Anthony Giddens (ed), *The Global Third Way Debate*, Polity 2001.

2   Tony Blair, *The Third Way*, Fabian Society 1998.

3   Commission for Taxation and Citizenship, *Paying for Progress: A New Politics of Tax for Public Spending*, Fabian Society 2000.

Paying for Progress
A New Politics of Tax for Public Spending

The Commission on Taxation and Citizenship

**Taxation—and the public spending it pays for—is the subject of the
fiercest political controversy.** *Paying for Progress: A New Politics of Tax* **for
Public Spending offers a compelling new approach.**

Reporting the results of new research into public attitudes towards taxation,
Paying for Progress argues that the public must be 'reconnected' to the taxes
they pay and the public services which these finance. To do this it proposes the
greater use of 'earmarked' taxes, including a new tax to fund the National Health
Service. Setting out a new philosophy of citzenship to underpin taxation policy,
it recommends a series of reforms to meet the goals of social inclusion and
environmental protection. And it asks: are higher taxes needed to pay for public
services?

Written in a lively and accessible style for the general reader, *Paying for Progress*
makes an important contribution to political thought and policy in the first
decade of the 21st century. Providing key information on the UK tax system, it
will also be an invaluable text for students and researchers in politics,
economics, public administration, law and accountancy.

'Coherent, radical and lucid... this important book raises critical questions for the
future of British politics'
Will Hutton, Chief Executive, the Industrial Society

'Highly recommended... The clarity with which it explores the facts and
arguments about the tax system make it an extremely valuable text for students
and researchers... it will provide a benchmark for future work on taxation
reform'
Andrew Gamble, Professor of Politics, University of Sheffield

November 2000 ■ ISBN 07163 6003 9 ■ £9.95

Coping with Post-democracy

Colin Crouch

'In this stimulating new pamphlet, Professor Colin Crouch makes links between the decline of the state and the waning of democratic enthusiasm. When so much of the public sector has been handed over to private operators, Crouch argues, what becomes of the image of government as a task that matters? If every public function is tested by its conformity with private-sector management goals, why should anyone get excited about choosing between parties? If government is routinely seen as incompetent, and the company as the only source of expertise, no wonder politics and democracy, in America if not yet here, are at an all-time low. This is a fate that Labour, not so long ago, would have been desperate to avoid ... At some stage, the Labour party may have to confront the lacuna that has been created on the left.'
Hugo Young, The *Guardian*

Colin Crouch is Professor of Sociology at the European University Institute, Florence, and External Scientific member of the Max Planck Institute for Society Research, Cologne

December 2000 ▪ ISBN 07163 0598 4 ▪ £6.95

Second Term Thinking

The Labour Party's historic election victory provides an unprecedented opportunity to develop a radical policy agenda. The Fabian Society's Second Term Thinking Series is intended to make a significant contribution to the development of innovative policy options across a range of areas. Second Term Thinking aims to stimulate debate both on the key strategic and philosophical directions of the post-election Government and the policies that will manifest them.

The titles published so far in this series of eight are:

A Level Playing Field: The Reform of Private Schools by **Harry Brighouse** which calls for change in the relationship between state and private education, harnessing private resources in the pursuit of equality of opportunity.
November 2000 ■ ISBN 07163 3052 0 ■ £7.50

Plugging the Parenting Gap: The Case for Paid Parental Leave by **Ruth Kelly** which demonstrates that paid parental leave could be a viable and popular policy.
June 2000 ■ ISBN 07163 3051 2 ■ £7.50

Votes for All: Compulsory Participation in Elections by **Tom Watson and Mark Tami** which makes the casse for compulsory voting in British elections.
February 2000 ■ ISBN 07163 3050 4 ■ £7.50

A Capital Idea: Start-Up Grants for Young People by **Julian Le Grand and David Nissan** which argues for a capital grant of £10,000 for all 18 year olds, as a springboard for opportunity.
February 2000 ■ ISBN 07163 3049 0 ■ £7.50

All eight titles are available for £30—please contact the Fabian Society on 020 7227 4900 or email bookshop@fabian-society.org.uk